The Economics of
Professional Team Sports

The Economics of Professional Team Sports

Henry G. Demmert
University of Santa Clara

Lexington Books
D.C. Heath and Company
Lexington, Massachusetts
Toronto   London

Library of Congress Cataloging in Publication Data

Demmert, Henry George.
   The economics of professional team sports.

   Bibliography: p.
   1. Sports–Economic aspects–United States.
I. Title. II. Title: Professional team sports.
GV716.D45   338.4'7'7960973   73-6605
ISBN 0-669-88161-9

International Standard Book Number: 0-669-88161-9

Library of Congress Catalog Card Number: 73-6605

Contents

v

List of Tables

Acknowledgments

My thanks go to Professors Richard Muth and Hayne E. Leland for their valuable suggestions, especially during the latter stages of this book.

I am also indebted to Mr. Len Shapiro and Mr. Wes Mathis of Sports Expert, Inc. of Santa Clara, California, for their help in sifting through the wealth of information contained in the Sports Expert library.

I am grateful to Miss Judy Lyding for her patience and efficiency in the preparation of the final manuscript.

My greatest debt by far is to Professor James N. Rosse whose guidance is largely responsible for whatever merit this book possesses.

Finally, to my wife, Susan, goes my everlasting gratitude for her devotion and forbearance during the past few years.

The Economics of
Professional Team Sports

1 Introduction

No one really believes that baseball isn't a business; not you or me or Anna Maria Alberghetti. What we really believe is that baseball is entitled to its special exemption because of its special character and the special position it holds in the national life. I go along with that. I also believe we could exist very nicely without the reserve clause, but that's another story.

Bill Veeck, former major league owner
and executive in *The Hustler's Handbook.*

This book applies economic analysis to an industry which neither closely fits any of the economist's traditional models of industrial structure, nor has been the subject of any intensive investigation by economists, and yet whose economic and institutional structure is the source of much current public controversy and concern. In particular, because of their preferential treatment under the antitrust statutes, certain overtly collusive activities are tolerated among the firms in this industry—more specifically among the firms in a league. These activities include extralegal restrictions on economic competition in both input and output markets in the form of the reserve system and territorial rights, respectively. The reserve system, which effectively eliminates interfirm bidding for the services of professional athletes, has the ostensible purpose of ensuring a relatively equal distribution of playing talent among the clubs in a league. Whether, in fact, any such constraints on player mobility are necessary to promote equality, and whether the particular institutions historically adopted can be expected to accomplish this, is a primary concern of our analysis. Recently, this question of the reserve system was before the United States Supreme Court in the form of a suit by a former major league baseball player, Curt Flood. Though the Court decided against Flood, its decision did little to resolve the controversy surrounding the reserve clause. Such resolution, the Court declared, should be left to the Congress.

In addition, stunned by the move of the Washington Senators baseball club from the nation's capital, and already in the midst of an investigation of the proposed merger between the American and National Basketball Associations, Congress has become increasingly concerned about the cartel structure of professional team sports. This structure is such that the league's franchising system effectively controls the total supply of the product, while its territorial rights provision makes each franchise a monopolist in its own market. These institutions and others which have important implications for the economic

1

analysis of the professional team sports industry are examined in detail in Chapter 2.

Although a few economists, among them Rottenberg [1956], Neal [1964], Jones [1969] and more recently El-Hodiri and Quirk [1971], have studied some economic aspects of the professional sports industy, none has successfully integrated economic analysis with its technological and institutional peculiarities in such a way as to produce a comprehensive model. In Chapters 3 and 4, therefore, we build upon these initial investigations in developing a model capable of explaining the behavior of professional sports clubs and also capable of establishing some tenable prescriptions for an enlightened public policy toward the industry. In Chapter 3 the main body of this model is developed and its implications with respect to relative playing strengths, the distribution of league profits, and the role of the reserve system are analyzed. In Chapter 4 a more formal model of team quality determination is constructed, and with the aid of a comparative statics approach, its implications for interclub variations in market strength are derived.

The model is then submitted to empirical evaluation in Chapter 5. A model of demand for attendance at major league baseball games is estimated in order to examine the relative effects on a club's revenues, and implicitly on its incentives, of fielding a winning team vis-à-vis maintaining league balance. In addition, a hypothesis regarding the effects on team quality of exogenous intermarket differences is tested, and the model is also evaluated in the light of some less formal evidence in the form of historical case studies.

In Chapter 6, the implications of the analysis for public policy are examined. Specifically, we first attempt to derive the market effects of a fully competitive structure, in both input and output markets, and finally suggestions are examined for a "second best" policy in which monopoly practices in output markets are assumed to be inevitable.

2

The Structure of the Professional Team Sports Industry: Some Institutional and Historical Background

Any attempt at an economic analysis of the professional team sports industry requires an understanding of its rather unique institutional framework. Indeed, as Neale [1964] has shown, it is from the peculiarities of this framework that the industry derives much of its interest as an object of investigation. This chapter, therefore, is devoted to a description of the salient structural and institutional characteristics of the market in which the services of professional team sports enterprises are exchanged.

Definition of the Industry

We restrict our attention to those firms or *clubs*[1] which field teams of "major league" quality in any of four sports: baseball, football, basketball, and hockey.[2] The generally accepted criterion for major league status in each of the above sports is membership respectively in either the National or American League of Professional Baseball Clubs (NL and AL), the National Football League (NFL), the National or American Basketball Associations (NBA or ABA), or the National Hockey League (NHL) or World Hockey Association (WHA). The two leagues in major league baseball are only nominally distinct. They are united by the Major League Agreement and, for the purposes of economic analysis, should be considered a single league. In basketball and hockey, however, the two leagues are economic competitors as of this writing.

The members of each of these leagues and associations are bound by a series of formal interfirm agreements dealing with the economic, sporting, and other aspects of their relationship. Thus, major league baseball may be defined as the set of all clubs subscribing to the Constitution of the National (or American) League of Professional Baseball Clubs, the Major League Agreement and some

---

[1] The words *firm* and *club* will be used interchangeably to refer to the production unit of this industry. The *team* will refer to the combination of various types of human capital, players, coaches, etc., which is a specific input in the productive process.

[2] This study excludes such professional sporting enterprises as prize fighting, golf, and tennis which are in general played as individual, rather than team, sports. Also excluded are such team "sports" as roller derby, where the legitimacy of the sporting competition is open to some question.

3

other, less important, documents. The structure of professional football, basketball, and hockey are outlined in analogous sets of contracts.[3]

Common to all of these agreements are constraints on the economic behavior of the individual clubs. These constraints will be discussed in detail below, since it is their effects, along with their rationale, that is a major concern of our analysis. Primary, though certainly not exclusive, emphasis will be on professional baseball, and this for two reasons: greater availability of information with respect to baseball and current questions of public policy regarding the sport's status.

Very few professional sports clubs are publicly held corporations. Ownership lies, for the most part, in the hands of private individuals, families, or closely held corporations, all of which are extremely reluctant to reveal the facts of their economic and financial operations. In trying unsuccessfully to obtain information on the revenues and expenses for a certain club, I was told by an executive of the club that, "There is certain information that simply cannot be made public." It was apparent from the context that the information referred to includes nearly anything that has to do with club finances. Other researchers in this area have been confronted with a similar predicament.[4]

There are, however, occasional exceptions to this general rule. In 1957 the Antitrust Subcommittee of the Committee on the Judiciary, House of Representatives, subpoenaed financial statements from most professional sports clubs, and those statements, covering the years 1952 through 1956, are available in the Hearings before that committee.[5] Also, *The Sporting News* and other newspapers often have access to enough information to make educated guesses about the magnitude of certain economic variables. Other researchers have found such data sufficiently accurate for their purposes.[6]

Table 2-1 shows the geographical and demographical distribution of professional sports firms in the United States. Nearly all[7] of the 35 most populous metropolitan areas in the United States have at least one professional club, and

[3]The constitutions of the American and National baseball leagues, the National Football League, the National Basketball Association and the National Hockey League may be found on pages 1394, 1417, 2580a, 2937, and 3009, respectively, of the Hearings Before the Antitrust Subcommittee of the Committee on the Judiciary, House of Representatives, 85th Cong., 1st Sess., Serial No. 8, Parts 1, 2, and 3: Organized Professional Team Sports. This will be hereafter designated as Hearings [1957].

[4]See, for example, the remarks of Koppet ([1967], pp. 158-59) and Davenport ([1969], p. 10). Even THE SPORTING NEWS, a publication most accurately described as the industry's trade journal, had to resort to "informed sources" in its attempt to analyze the financial structure of professional team sports. See, "Sports Rank as a High Risk Investment" by Vito Stellino, THE SPORTING NEWS, May 8, 1971.

[5]Hearings [1957].

[6]See, for example, Pascal and Rapping [1970], p. 16.

[7]If some reasonable leeway is allowed in defining metropolitan areas (namely, including Newark and Paterson, N.J., in the New York metropolitan area, San Jose in the San Francisco area, and Riverside-San Bernardino in the Los Angeles-Long Beach area), then only Tampa-St. Petersburg, Florida, and Columbus, Ohio, among the 35 most populous areas are without a major professional sports franchise.

Table 2-1
Geographical/Demographical Distribution of Major Professional Sports Franchise

Population Rank	Metropolitan Area	Baseball	Football	Basketball	Hockey	Total
1	New York, NY	2	2	2	3	9
2	Los Angeles, CA	1	1	1	2	5
3	Chicago, IL	2	1	1	2	6
4	Philadelphia, PA	1	1	1	2	5
5	Detroit, MI	1	1	1	1	4
6	Boston, MA	1	1	1	2	5
7	San Francisco–Oakland, CA	2	2	1	1	6
8	Washington, D.C.	X	1	X	X	1
9	Pittsburg, PA	1	1	1	1	4
10	St. Louis, MO	1	1	X	1	3
11	Cleveland, OH	1	1	1	1	4
12	Baltimore, MD	1	1	1	X	3
13	Newark, NJ	X	X	X	X	X
14	Houston, TX	1	1	1	1	4
15	Minneapolis, MN	1	1	X	2	4
16	Dallas, TX	1	1	1	X	3
17	Cincinnati, OH	1	1	1	X	3
18	Milwaukee, WI	1	1	1	X	3
19	Buffalo, NY	X	1	1	1	3
20	Paterson, NJ	X	X	X	X	X
21	Atlanta, GA	1	1	1	1	4
22	Seattle, WA	X	X	1	X	2
23	Kansas City, MO	1	1	X	X	2
24	San Diego, CA	1	1	1	X	3
25	Anaheim, CA	1	X	X	X	1
26	Miami, FL	X	1	1	X	2
27	Denver, CO	X	1	1	X	2
28	New Orleans, LA	X	1	X	X	1
30	Indianapolis, IN	X	X	1	X	1
32	Portland, OR	X	X	1	X	1
35	Phoenix, AZ	X	X	1	X	1
43	Memphis, TN	X	X	1	X	1
60	Salt Lake City, UT	X	X	1	X	1
Regional Franchises						
	Carolina	X	X	1	X	1
	Kentucky	X	X	1	X	1
	Virginia	X	X	1	X	1
Canada						
	Montreal	1	X	X	1	2

Table 2-1 (cont.)

Population Rank	Metropolitan Area	Baseball	Football	Basketball	Hockey	Total
	Toronto	X	X	X	1	1
	Vancouver	X	X	X	1	1
	Winnepeg	X	X	X	1	1
	Ottawa	X	X	X	1	1
	Quebec	X	X	X	1	1
	Alberta	X	X	X	1	1

nearly all of the first 20 have at least three.[8] Several franchises of the relatively new American Basketball Association have not confined themselves to a single metropolitan area. Faced with the dilemma of competing with the established NBA (and NHL) in the major cities, or satisfying themselves with the less populous remaining markets, some ABA clubs have opted to expand their home markets to statewide operations in Virginia, Kentucky, and the Carolinas.[9] Their schedules call for the teams to play a number of games in each of the major population centers of the respective states.

The geographical diversity apparent from Table 2-1 has not always been the case. During the last twenty years, especially during the past decade, the industry has simultaneously expanded and shifted its geographical center westward and southward. Prior to 1958, there were a total of only 41 major professional team sports franchises in 19 cities stretched along the population belt from the Great Lakes to the Northeastern Seaboard. By 1973 the industry had expanded to the 105 clubs distributed throughout most of the United States and Canada, and the number of scheduled professional athletic contests had risen from fewer than 2,000 to more than 4,000 per year.

Assets and Returns

The pronounced increase in the number of clubs would seem to indicate the presence of high rates of return on capital invested in the industry. The fact that barriers to entry are quite formidable serves to strengthen this impression.[10] However, the tendency toward secrecy on the part of the clubs makes substantiation difficult. Furthermore, questionable accounting practices make calculation of returns difficult even when details of the financial structure are

[8] All 20, in fact, do, if we recognize Baltimore and Washington, D.C., as a single metropolitan area. Their physical proximity allows this as reasonable.

[9] ABA clubs were, in fact, forced out of the Los Angeles, San Francisco-Oakland, and Washington-Baltimore areas where they faced economic competition from established NBA clubs. At present, New York is the only market shared by clubs from the two leagues.

[10] The nature and magnitude of these barriers to entry is discussed below.

made public.[11] Given these words of caution, the evidence that is available is still somewhat instructive.

The behavior of the market values of various franchises is enlightening when inquiring into the true profit picture of the firms in the professional sports industry. The assets of a major professional sports franchise consist primarily of player contacts, territorial (monopoly) rights, official recognition as "major league," and certain units of physical capital such as an arena or stadium. The recent behavior of these asset values as shown in Table 2-2 suggests the existence of substantial rates of return. Owners and executives of the various franchises, however, invariably portray themselves not as businessmen but as "sportsmen" forced to endure yearly financial losses for the "good of the game." This approach to public relations often leads to the necessity for incredible public utterances in the face of apparently contradictory evidence.[12] For example, one owner of an NFL club claims that, "The money in pro football is not in profits, . . . the gains . . . in the game come from appreciation in the value of the franchise."[13] Another owner, however, admits that, though, "It's awfully hard to make money in this game, . . . I've never heard of anybody losing any either."[14]

As Table 2-2 shows, the latter statement seems more in line with the recent behavior of the market values of professional sports clubs. All but one of the franchises listed have appreciated in value, some substantially, over the period listed.

In addition, the most recent expansion clubs have generally been auctioned at much higher prices than were the expansion teams of a decade ago, in spite of the fact that most of the newer franchises are located in market areas which, a

---

[11] See, for example, the analysis by Noll and Okner ([1971], pp. 32-36) and the comments by Davenport ([1969], p. 11) on the peculiar accounting practices employed by certain baseball clubs. Koppet ([1967], pp. 159-60) also gives an illuminating example of the effects of varying accounting methods pointing out that, for the year 1956, the Boston Red Sox baseball club reported in the Hearings [1957] a positive net income of $122,032. Separately, the *same* club for the *same* year reported in THE SPORTING NEWS a *loss* of $616,640.

[12] For some of the inconsistencies in this "good of the game" facade as an approach to public relations in major league baseball see Flood [1971], especially Chapter 4, "Geniuses Need Not Apply."

[13] Ralph Wilson, owner of the Buffalo Bills of the NFL, as quoted in Davenport [1969], p. 11. It apparently never occurred to Mr. Wilson to question how a money losing operation, not acquiring any new physical assets, could appreciate in value over time. An editorial in THE SPORTING NEWS (May 8, 1971, p. 14) attempts to reconcile the contradictory evidence but only succeeds in showing that professional sports franchises can generate indirect "profits" through such things as "advertising-like" benefits and tax savings.

[14] Joseph Iglehart, President of the Baltimore Orioles, as quoted in Davenport [1969], p. 11.

Table 2-2

Some Recent Changes in the Asset Value of Professional Sports Clubs*

Franchise and League	Sport	Year	Estimated Value or Selling Price	Year	Estimated Value or Selling Price	Average Yearly Percentage Change in Value
Seattle/Milwaukee, AL	Baseball	1969	5.6	1970	10.8	+92.9
Milwaukee, AL	Baseball	1970	10.8	1971	11.0	+ 1.9
Kansas City, AL	Baseball	1954	3.5	1964	3.0	– 1.4
Kansas City–Oakland, AL	Baseball	1964	3.0	1971	8.0	+23.8
Kansas City, AL	Baseball	1969	6.0	1971	7.5	+12.5
New York, AL	Baseball	1945	2.8	1964	14.0	+21.0
New York, AL	Baseball	1964	14.0	1970	16.0	+ 2.4
New York, NL	Baseball	1962	3.75	1971	20.0	+48.1
Cincinnati, NL	Baseball	1962	2.0	1966	6.0	+50.0
Buffalo, NFL	Football	1959	1.4	1966	10.0	+98.0
Philadelphia, NFL	Football	1964	5.5	1969	16.0	+38.2
San Diego, NBA	Basketball	1968	2.0	1971	5.6	+60.0
Boston, NBA	Basketball	1965	2.8	1969	6.2	+30.4

*Source: "Who Says Baseball Is Like Ballet," FORBES, April 1, 1971, p. 30 and "Sports Rank as a High Risk Investment," by Vito Stellini, THE SPORTING NEWS, May 8, 1971, p. 42.

priori, generally would be less attractive than those acquired in earlier expansions. In 1962, for example, New York and Houston interests paid $3.75 million and $5 million, respectively, for the right to field baseball teams in the National League. In 1969, investors in Montreal and San Diego paid $10 million each for the same right.[15] In 1960 the then new Dallas and Minnesota National Football League clubs cost $6 million each. The entry of Atlanta and New Orleans into the NFL eight years later was at a cost of $8.5 million per franchise.

According to Noll and Okner [1971], a majority of professional basketball teams are losing money. Yet in the NBA the new franchises in Cleveland, Portland, and Buffalo brought $3.7 million each in 1970, while the expansion franchise in Phoenix had cost $2 million two years before.

In major league baseball, even the American League, with its much publicized financial troubles,[16] still finds that its expansion franchises command at least what they did a decade ago.

It is more difficult to obtain information on the value of separate components of the assets which comprise the major league franchise. The largest part of the purchase price of an expansion club is for the right to "draft" players' contracts from the rosters of existing teams—in effect the cost of obtaining the playing talent necessary to field a team. The nominal recognition of major league status is also of considerable value. This might explain why each team in the fledgling American Basketball Association has agreed to pay a $1.25 million "indemnity" to the NBA should the Congress approve their merger plan. The quality of play in the ABA is generally considered to be inferior to that in the NBA, and official recognition of the ABA as a major league (via its participation in a World Championship playoff) would considerably enhance its image and its financial stability. It is interesting to note that the above "indemnity"is equal to more than one-third the original market value of the most recent (1970) NBA expansion franchises.

Davenport [1969] attempted to calculate rates of return for the Baltimore baseball club, a club that is a moderately successful member of the American League. He gave the club the benefit of the doubt on some of its rather dubious accounting procèdures and still arrived at a rate of return fluctuating from 10 or 11 percent in "bad years" to upwards of 25 percent in "good years." It is interesting to note that over the four year period considered by Davenport, Baltimore's average yearly attendance was 969,000, only 35,000 more than the average for the American League as a whole. Furthermore, Baltimore's other major revenue source, broadcast rights, has typically been below the league average. This indicates a healthier profit picture than baseball owners typically like to portray for themselves.

With respect to professional basketball, Noll and Okner [1971] attempt to

---

[15]"Who Says Baseball Is Like Ballet?" FORBES, April 1, 1971, pp. 24-31.

[16]The FORBES article cited above claims that 7 of 12 American League clubs experienced deficits in 1970.

calculate profit rates for the Milwaukee Bucks. They contend that the Bucks rank third among NBA clubs in profitability, behind New York and Los Angeles, and that their long run rate of profit is at least 17 percent and probably closer to 22 percent. (The latter, higher, figure takes into account the fact that much of what is really pure profit is entered as an expense, since it accrues to the owner-managers of the firm in the form of inflated salaries.)

The Product and Its Implications for Revenue

The largest source of income for any major league club arises from the sale, either via tickets or broadcast rights, of its primary product, the game or match. The product is unique in that it cannot be produced by a single firm, but only by combining the inputs (specifically, the teams) of two sportingly competitive firms.[17] The stream of utility arising from the match (or the dimensions of its quality) can be divided into three parts: First there is uncertainty of outcome—the concept of an athletic contest. This aspect of the match's quality presumably is positively related to the degree of uncertainty associated with any given match. The closer the two teams in overall quality, the more attractive is the match to the potential ticket buyer or television viewer.

A second aspect of the match is its entertainment value. This is distinct from uncertainty of outcome and may exist quite apart from the latter.[18] A game may be very attractive to the potential consumer, even though he expects it to be a mismatch from the standpoint of athletic competition. The potential reasons for this are numerous. They can be related to the nature of the particular sport; to social, cultural, or ethnic considerations;[19] to the participation of an attractive personality;[20] to the possibility of a record breaking performance; and so on.

Finally, the strong association between a winning team and substantial ticket sales indicates that consumers obtain utility from the vicarious pleasure of

---

[17]Neale ([1964], p. 2) refers somewhat facetiously to this attribute of the product as the "Inverted Joint Product or the Product Joint."

[18]The FORBES ([1971], p. 26) article cited above quotes Bill Veeck, an ex-owner of major and minor league baseball franchises, on this aspect of the product and how it relates to baseball's alleged financial difficulties: "What football managements have learned to do . . . is sell the game itself as exciting. Even if a contest isn't for the Super Bowl title, people will watch to plot the strategy, see a good pass or a bonejarring tackle. Baseball, on the other hand, has sold the won-and-loss column. A team almost has to be in contention for the penant to rate a good audience . . ."

[19]The rapid rise in the popularity of professional football, for example, has often been related to the increasing violence (or awareness thereof) in our society. See the comment by Dr. Joyce Brothers as quoted in FORBES [1971], p. 26.

[20]See, for example, Davenport's ([1969], pp. 17-18) interesting calculation of the effects of the pitcher, Sandy Koufax, on attendance at Los Angeles Dodger baseball games.

relating to a winner. There are a few counterexamples to this general observation—most notably the New York Met phenomenon of the mid-1960s—but, *ceteris paribus*, a potential audience would rather identify with a winning team than with a losing one, and will pay for that opportunity.

The following figures are meant to be suggestive rather than a formal test of this contention. Taking major league baseball's 1971 season as a sample, teams were classified as "Good" if they were leading their division or were a very close second, and as "Poor" if they were in last or second to last place and clearly out of pennant contention. For a random sample of "Good" and "Poor" teams, paid attendance was observed for "Good" teams' home games against "Poor" teams, home games against other "Good" teams, and so on. The results (with the number of games in the sample in parentheses) are given in the following table.

Home Team

		Good	Poor
Visiting	Good	24,610 (42)	11,349 (35)
Team	Poor	16,066 (32)	9,806 (43)

Note where uncertainty of outcome is most lacking (the off diagonal entries), the home team attracts substantially more attendance (16,066) if it is the a priori probable winner, than if it is the probable loser (11,349).[21]

The product or match is a direct source of revenue to the club via the sale of tickets to a live audience, on either a seasonal or a game-by-game basis. There is, of course, a physical limit to the number of tickets that can be sold for any given match, namely, the seating capacity of the arena in which it is held. The effectiveness of this constraint varies from sport to sport and from club to club within any given sport, but it appears to be binding most often in hockey and least often in baseball. Neither the Montreal Canadiens nor the Toronto Maple Leafs of the NHL, for example, has played to less than 100 percent of capacity in their home arenas in over 20 years.[22] On the other hand, the 1963 Los Angeles Dodgers established the seasonal record for major league baseball attendance averaging only slightly better than 60 percent of capacity in their large stadium. The Boston Red Sox managed to fill their stadium, one of the smallest in major league baseball, to a record average of 73 percent of capacity in 1968. Most baseball clubs rarely play to capacity crowds.

---

[21] See Jones ([1969], p. 6) on the effect of winning on ticket demand in professional hockey.

[22] Jones [1969], p. 8. Unless these clubs have estimated their demand functions so accurately that they can set a price which exactly clears their capacity (a highly unlikely event), it seems that their tickets are underpriced. These firms are quite concerned about maintaining consumer "goodwill" and are reluctant to change their admission prices very often or by very much. In addition, the clubs have expanded their arena capacity over this period, Montreal by nearly 50 percent.

Another major source of revenue arising from the production of a match is the sale of broadcast rights to radio and television. These rights are usually sold as seasonal packages rather than on a game-by-game basis, and the seller may be the individual club, the league, or a combination of the two. In general, the revenues arising from league sale of broadcasting rights are divided equally among the clubs in the league.

The relative importance of television as a revenue source has increased faster in the past decade for football, basketball, and hockey than it has for baseball. Television (and to a lesser extent, radio) is, of course, a partial substitute for in-person attendance, and although the marginal cost (to the club) of increasing the number of telecasts is probably close to zero, it may not pay a club to televise all of its games because of the adverse effect this would have on ticket sales. The relevant cross elasticities in the demand function must, therefore, be taken into account in determining the optimal number of broadcasts.

Other parameters of telecasts, besides their number, are also important. Cross elasticities between in-person attendance and television audience generally are presumably larger for home games than they are for road games and, hence, the number of road games a club will televise is usually greater than the number of home games. The cross-elasticity also varies inversely with the radius of the broadcast, thus often leading clubs to establish a "blackout" policy with respect to their immediate market areas.

Even parameters of a telecast itself can affect the cross elasticities. The New York Mets, for example, felt it necessary to control the number of "instant replays" shown in the telecasts of their home games, fearing that an excessive number of replays has an adverse effect on home attendance and total revenue.[23]

A third source of revenue for the typical club is from concessions (parking, food, etc.). This income source is closely related to total home attendance, and it may be considered as complementary to in-person attendance.

Finally, the club may augment its income through the sale of players' contracts, marketing rights to club emblems, and rental of a stadium or arena to other users.

A numerical breakdown of these revenue sources is given in Table 2-3. The estimates given for 1952 and 1956 are league averages calculated from the data supplied to Congress and reproduced in the Hearings [1957].

In addition Koppet ([1967], pp. 160-61) has provided us with his estimates of the revenue breakdown of a "successful (baseball) club in a large city, like New York, Chicago or Los Angeles." He was writing in 1967 and his estimates

---

[23] See "Cut-back in Slow Motion Replays," by Jack Craig, THE SPORTING NEWS, July 24, 1971, p. 13. Anyone who has recently attended a sporting event, watched a spectacular play and found himself awaiting the "instant replay" only to be disappointed, can testify to the effect of this broadcast parameter on the substitutability between live attendance and television viewing.

Table 2-3

Some Estimates of Revenues and Costs for Major League Sports Clubs (Dollar Amounts are in Thousands)

	A. Revenues							
	1952		1956		1967		Most Recent	
	$	%	$	%	$	%	$	%
A. Baseball								
Home Attendance	1060	54.5	1450	54.8	330	55.0	3000	44.8
Road Attendance	240	12.3	292	11.0	600	10.0	600	9.0
Radio/TV	260	13.4	451	17.0	900	15.0	1700	25.4
Concessions	195	10.0	260	9.8	600	10.0	700	10.4
Other	190	9.8	195	7.4	600	10.0	700	10.4
Total	1945	100.0	2648	100.0	6000	100.0	6700	100.0
B. Football								
Home Attendance	360	47.5	470	45.6				
Road Attendance	164	21.6	225	21.9				
Exhibitions	127	16.8	158	15.3				
Radio/TV	70	9.2	143	13.9			1500	35.7
Concessions	7	0.9	6	0.6				
Other	30	4.0	27	2.6				
Total	758	100.0	1029	100.0			4200	100.0
C. Basketball								
Ticket Sales	174	78.0	220	81.0				
Exhibitions	19	8.5	14	5.1				
Radio/TV	17	7.6	20	7.4				
Concessions	3	1.4	3	1.1				
Other	10	4.5	15	5.5				
Total	223	100.0	272	100.0			2000	
D. Hockey (NHL only)								
Ticket Sales	364	87.6	459	90.0				
Exhibitions	21	5.1	20	4.0				
Radio/TV	26	6.3	25	5.0				
Concessions	0	0.0	0	0.0				
Other	4	1.0	5	1.0				
Total	415	100.0	509	100.0			2400	

	B. Operating Expenses					
	1952		1956		Most Recent	
	$	%	$	%	$	%
A. Baseball						
Player Salaries	417	24.0	463	21.6	1000	18.2
Other	1320	76.0	1682	78.4	4500	81.8
Total	1737	100.0	2145	100.0	5500	100.0

Table 2-3 (cont.)

			B. Operating Expenses			
	1952		1956		Most Recent	
B. Football						
Player Salaries	260	36.5	316	33.8	1100	29.3
Other	452	63.5	618	66.2	2650	70.7
Total	712	100.0	934	100.0	3750	100.0
C. Basketball						
Player Salaries	76	32.6	103	40.0	750	50.0
Other	157	67.4	155	60.0	750	50.0
Total	233	100.0	258	100.0	1500	100.0
D. Hockey (NHL only)						
Player Salaries	169	36.0	190	35.2	750	45.5
Other	300	64.0	349	64.8	900	54.5
Total	469	100.0	539	100.0	1650	100.0

appear in that column in Table 2-3. In the columns labelled "Most Recent," I have attempted to piece together the fragmentary evidence available and to estimate some revenue and cost components. The starting points are two articles which recently appeared in *The Sporting News*.[24] According to these sources total income for baseball in 1970 was around $160 million, for football, $110 million, for basketball, $55 million, and for hockey, $33 million. The estimated costs of operating a major league franchise for a year are about $5-$6 million, $3.5-$4 million, $1-$2 million, and $1.5-$1.8 million, respectively, for the four sports. Starting with these figures and adding other available information, the last column in the table was "guesstimated."

Another aspect of the industry's product, and one which is primarily external to the production process of any individual club, is the *pennant race* or, as Neale [1964] refers to it, the *league standings effect*. Just as the match or game is jointly produced by any two teams, the pennant race must be produced jointly by all teams in the league, but in this case, it is not directly marketable by any of them. Rather, its role is analogous to that of advertising, in that the existence of a close race is thought to increase the demand for seats at a match and broadcast rights.[25] The pennant race also generates a stream of utility for

[24]Stellini [1971], and "Sports Payrolls Examined," THE SPORTING NEWS, April 8, 1972, p. 46.

[25]The pennant race generates advertising in an even more direct sense via what Neale calls the "fourth estate benefit." A close pennant race tends to increase the demand for newspaper coverage of the games and their effects on league standings. This is an external benefit to the newspaper industry, but also provides advertising to the sports industry. See Neale [1964], p. 3.

those consumers who enjoy following the daily or weekly changes in the positions of the teams within a league. This good itself is not marketable and, hence, must be thought of as a social, or public, good.

These then are the dimensions of the product sold by the club: uncertainty of outcome, entertainment, association with a winning team, and the balance of competition within the league. We can think of these as the quality parameters of the firm's primary product, the match or schedule of matches, which generates revenue by the direct sale of two substitute goods—tickets and broadcast rights.

The externalities and interdependencies in this production process have important implications for joint behavior on the part of the clubs within a league. We, therefore, turn to an investigation of the league as an institution for collective decisions.

The League and Collective Activity

Due to the unique nature of the production process, all clubs are members of joint associations or leagues, wherein they are bound by a set of formal, extralegal agreements. The substance of these agreements constitutes a cartel organization among the clubs within a league. Neale ([1964], p. 4) has suggested that the "firm" in professional sports is the league, rather than the individual club; but it is more fruitful for this research to look upon the league as a collective body, the objectives of whose members may, and often do, conflict.

Each of the individual clubs has equal representation within the league, and the clubs themselves are the sole source of the league's power. The commissioner, or the league president, wields no decision-making authority other than in routine matters. Speaking specifically of major league baseball, Koppet contends that, "*No one* but an owner has any real power in baseball. . . . The commissioner, theoretically, is at the top of the baseball structure, but in reality he is the *employee* of the owners, and anytime one loses sight of that fact, one loses his ability to comprehend clearly what is happening in baseball."[26] Individual clubs are presumably bound by the decisions of the collective body, but they also participate in the making of those decisions. The league itself has no authority which transcends that of the owners.

The collective decision rules usually require more than a simple majority vote of the individual clubs for approval of a measure and, in some important decisions such as league expansion, unanimity may be required.

Most joint activity of the clubs within a league falls into one of three categories: (1) Activities dealing with the production and standardization of the

---

[26] Koppet [1967], p. 217. Italics Koppet's. See also his Appendix III, "The Baseball Hierarchy," for an outline of the structure of the collective decision-making apparatus in major league baseball.

product, (2) activities dealing with the public image of the sport, and (3) activities dealing with the economic interdependencies among the clubs in the league. In the first category are decisions concerning scheduling, rule changes and so forth, which arise from the nature of the product and the production process. These do not concern us here.

Collective activities regarding the public image of the sport are mainly concerned with safeguarding the integrity of athletic competition. Any activities which may in any way, however remotely, be connected with "point shaving" or "fixing" contests are dealt with harshly (and publicly) by the commissioner.[27] Professional sports sometimes try to regulate even the life styles of the players, again, for the "good of the game" as the owners perceive it. In fact, a player's contract always contains a section on "Club Rules and Regulations" which, among other things, may forbid the drinking of intoxicants and prescribe norms of dress in public.[28] These "public image" actions on the part of the league are also only tangential to our research.

Of major import, however, are joint actions dealing with the economic aspects of firm interdependencies—those collective decisions which in effect make the industry a cartel. Such explicitly collusive activities as are permitted among professional sports clubs would certainly be in violation of antitrust statutes were they to occur in any other type of enterprise. Indeed, the treatment of this industry by the courts and the Congress has represented something less than a scrupulous application of the antitrust laws.[29]

The special status of the industry began with the ruling in 1922 in *Federal Baseball Club v. National League* wherein the Supreme Court ruled that baseball was neither interstate nor commerce and, hence, was not subject to the antitrust laws.[30] Later, in *Toolson v. New York Yankees* (1953), the Court upheld its earlier decision and added that "Congress had no intention of including baseball within the scope of the federal antitrust laws." Yet one year earlier, the Celler Subcommittee on the Study of Monopoly Power had concluded that "the Congress has the jurisdiction to investigate and legislate on the subject of professional baseball." Note that the Court had not yet ruled on the applicability or nonapplicability of the antitrust laws to professional sports other than

---

[27]All players involved in the infamous "Black Sox" scandal in 1919 were expelled from professional baseball for life. More recently such established NFL stars as Paul Hornung and Alex Karras (1965) have been suspended, and Joe Namath (1970) threatened with suspension for mere alleged association with suspected gambling elements.

[28]Hearings Before the Subcommittee on Antitrust and Monopoly of the Committee on the Judiciary, United States Senate, 88th Cong., 2nd. Sess. Pursuant to S. Res. 262 on S. 2391 (1964), p. 205. Hereafter referred to as Hearings [1964].

[29]The situation is quite similar with respect to the status of the National Hockey League in Canada. See Jones [1969], p. 1.

[30]This brief legal history is based upon the statement of Leslie M. O'Connor which appears in the Hearings [1964], pp. 354-384. Mr. O'Connor is an attorney and a past president of the Pacific Coast League.

baseball, and the responsibility for the dissolution of this inconsistency was assigned to the Congress when in *Radovich v. National Footbal League* (1957) the Court held that "legislation, not court decision, is the orderly way to eliminate error or discrimination which may arise from the Supreme Court decisions that organized baseball is not, but other similar sports are, within the scope of federal antitrust laws." It is apparent from this context that the Court was referring to the "error" of the *Federal Baseball* decision.

Armed with this ruling Congress has from time to time tried to eliminate the inconsistencies with regard to the antitrust status of professional sports. Inconclusive hearings were held in the summer of 1957 and again in the winter of 1964 on the Hart Bill. The latter would have explicitly exempted all professional sports from the antitrust laws in four areas: (1) Equalization of athletic competition within a league, (2) rights to operate exclusively in, that is, to monopolize, a geographic area, (3) employment practices, and (4) preservation of public confidence in the honesty of the sport.[31] It has always been the contention of the club owners and their spokesmen, the commissioners, that such preferred treatment under the law is absolutely essential for the economic viability of the industry.

At the urging of the club owners the Hart Bill cleared committee and, according to Veeck[1965], approval appeared likely until—nine days later—the Columbia Broadcasting System purchased the New York Yankees, whereupon Rep. Emmanuel Celler withdrew his support of the measure. According to one observer, "The Supreme Court exemption was based upon its considered opinion that baseball is a sport rather than an entertainment. . . . Celler seemed to have grave doubts whether baseball was lending any particular aid and comfort to this legal illusion by bringing the world's greatest merchandiser of entertainment into the fold."[32] With the failure of the Hart Bill, the legal status of professional team sports remains muddled and inconsistent.

Since certain collective aspects of club behavior that have aroused controversy with respect to their antitrust status are a major concern of this book, it is necessary to examine them in some detail. Except as otherwise noted, each of these applies to all of the four sports under consideration.

League enforcement of *territorial rights* constitutes it as a market-sharing cartel. These rights establish each club as a monopoly seller of its particular service in its assigned market.[33] No other club may perform in that market, either directly or via broadcast, unless the team with territorial rights tempo-

---

[31] Hearings [1964], pp. 2-3. It is also interesting to note that the Bill's sponsor, Senator Hart of Michigan, is a son-in-law of the late owner of the Detroit Tigers baseball club. See Veeck [1965], p. 63.

[32] Veeck [1965], p. 65. According to Veeck, Celler not only withdrew his support, but urged an antitrust suit against baseball.

[33] Exceptions may occur in some of the larger markets. For example, there are two baseball clubs in New York and Chicago. Even when this is the case, cross elasticities between the two may be relatively small, especially in the short run as suggested by Veeck [1965], p. 167.

rarily waives them. The degree of monopoly power which this bestows upon any given club depends upon a number of market parameters. These include the existence and quality of other professional sports clubs in the market and the availability of alternative forms of entertainment. Since the market is divided among the various sports on a temporal basis (with the exception of the hockey-basketball season and other minor overlaps), the second of these may be of relatively greater importance. This is especially true for baseball whose spring and summer season also provides its potential audience with a plentiful supply of alternative leisure-time activities. In fact, the Commissioner of baseball has recently declared, "I'm not so worried about (other) competitive sports as I am the struggle with other summer activities for the entertainment dollar."[34] The other sports of course face similar competition, but given their seasons, the potential audience is probably not confronted with as wide an array of substitute activities.

Entry into the league and hence the size of the industry and the total supply of the product, is also determined by the league cartel. In general, it takes unanimous approval by all member clubs for the league to grant a new franchise. Thus, entry into the industry can be accomplished in one of two ways: Either the new franchise is purchased from the existing league at a price high enough to induce all of the established clubs to agree to expand, or the potential entrant must establish his own league. The latter course of action requires the commitment of large sums of capital, by a number of independent investors, to what has in the past proven to be a highly risky venture. The recent success of the ABA must be tempered by the realization that two previous attempts to challenge the monopoly position of the NBA failed. Similarly, the acceptance of the AFL into the NFL football monopoly followed prior unsuccessful attempts at setting up an independent professional football league in the postwar period Given the monopoly position of the league, the highly differentiated product, the occupation of nearly all prime markets by existing clubs, and the apparent risk accompanying any challenge to this monopoly structure, it is not reasonable to characterize entry barriers as substantial.

The pricing decisions are made by the individual clubs rather than by the league cartel. Ticket prices are announced prior to the start of the season and, even in the face of unforeseen shifts in demand, are not usually altered over its course.[35] Demand shifts often occur as a result of such things as injuries to key players, rapid development of newer players, and unexpected position in the league standings.

In general, tickets are priced according to the "quality" of the seat being sold.

[34] Bowie Kuhn, as quoted in "Who Says Baseball Is Like Ballet?" FORBES, April, 1971, p. 26.

[35] There have been a few minor exceptions to this in the past. The Boston Red Sox, for example, set two prices for certain classes of seats. One price would be considered the normal one and the other was announced as the price to be charged when a large crowd was expected. The Pittsburg Pirates had a slightly different price schedule for weekends than they had for weekday games.

This "quality," however, is defined by the club and may be a decision variable. It is common practice, for example, for a club to nominally reclassify groups of seats, say from "general admission" to higher priced "reserved," thereby increasing the average price of its product without actually announcing price changes.[36] Some clubs also practice a limited amount of third-degree price discrimination when different markets can be identified and separated. Different prices are often charged children, students, the military, and other easily distinguishable groups whose demand elasticities presumably are higher than average.

The real price of a ticket is also often reduced by the club's promotional and "give-away" activities. This is particularly true in baseball where there is much unused capacity which can be supplied at, or near, zero marginal cost. Such things as "Bat Day," "Cap Day," Ladies Night" and so on, are usually scheduled for a club's otherwise unattractive home dates against a poor team. They are designed to appeal to groups, such as women and children, whose members will most likely be accompanied by a paying customer. This type of promotional activity is comparatively rare in football and hockey where unused capacity is not so prevalent.

The division of ticket revenues between home and visiting teams, the problem of *gate shares*, is another area subject to collective decision. This, of course, has a pronounced effect on the distribution of revenues in a league whose member clubs are located in markets of varying potential. The smaller the visitor's share of gate revenues, the greater the effect of intermarket variations on the revenue functions of the individual clubs. The implications of this observation will be developed more fully below.

The actual division of gate shares varies considerably from sport to sport. In basketball and hockey the visiting club receives no share of the gate.[37] In baseball[38] the split gives about 20 percent to the visiting team after allowance for taxes, the treatment of season tickets, league shares, and other factors.[39] Football, on the other hand, uses a 60-40 split and the result is greater equality of NFL clubs with respect to revenue potential. Indeed, it is not unheard of for an NFL club to have greater revenues on the road than at home. Davenport ([1969], p. 10) claims that this was the case for the Dallas Cowboys in 1963.

---

[36] The fact is emphasized that owners try to subordinate the business aspects of their product to the sporting aspects.

[37] Actually, six percent of the gate in the NBA is retained by the league to be distributed among clubs which qualify for the championship playoffs.

[38] For a long time teams in major league baseball received a flat sum per admission. As the average ticket price began to rise, the percent share of the gate going to the visiting team, of course, fell. Not until 1965 did the American League finally adopt a 20 percent rule for the visitors share of admissions. The National League still pays the visiting team a flat 27-1/2 cents per paid admission. See Koppet [1967], p. 161.

[39] See Koppet ([1967], p. 162) for a discussion of the effect of advance sale of season tickets on the actual gate division.

Radio and television revenues also fall under the potential regulation of the league. In general, radio revenues are negotiated by the individual club in its own market and, hence, these will vary considerably from club to club within any given sport, being more lucrative in the more populous markets.

The treatment of television revenues is of more interest. Each of the leagues has a contract with at least one major network to televise some portion of its games on a nationwide scale.[40] The revenues from league sale of telecast rights are divided equally among the clubs in the league. In addition, in all sports but football, individual clubs may independently sell rights for telecasts within their own market area, usually to a nonnetwork station.

The revenue potential of this source to a club is directly related to the population and other demographic characteristics of its market, and as such these revenues vary considerably from firm to firm. For example, the average major league baseball team receives about $1 million for its independently negotiated radio-television rights, but the range in 1973, as reported by *The Sporting News* (March 24, 1973, p. 42) is from $1.8 million (Los Angeles Dodgers) to $0.6 million (Milwaukee Brewers). Assuming an equal split of network television money of about $18 million, the average major league baseball team received approximately $1.8 million in radio-television revenues in 1972, with a range of about $1.4 million to $2.55 million. Each NFL club received about $1.5 million in television money alone in 1970, but the money was divided equally among all 26 teams in the league.

The Market for Athletic Talent

The input market for playing talent is perhaps the most cartelized aspect of the league's economic operations.[41] A series of interfirm agreements, dealing with the employment of players and their distribution among the teams in the league, is such that each club is established as a potential discriminating monopsonist with respect to the purchase of athletic talent. The avowed purpose of most of these labor market institutions is to insure equality of playing strengths among the various clubs. An analysis of the effects of, and the need for, these institutions is central to this book, and their structure must be examined in some detail.

The *reserve clause*, in effect in one form or another in every professional sports league in the United States, is a provision in each player's contract giving the club with which he has contracted an exclusive option on the renewal of that

---

[40] Major league baseball has its contract with NBC, the NBA with ABC, the NHL with CBS, and the NFL with all three major networks. A 1961 law allows a professional sports league to act as a monopoly seller of television (and radio) rights as the agent of all the members of the league.

[41] See Rottenberg [1956] for a thorough discussion of this.

contract. It precludes any other club in the league from bidding for his services and at the same time forbids his offering those services to any other club in the league at any price. Even if he retires, his contract is still the property of the last club that owned it, and he cannot return to the league except to play for that club.

In baseball and hockey the club's option is permanent—if the player ever wants to play professional baseball, he must play for the club that owns his contract, convince that club to sell or trade the contract to another club, or buy the contract himself. In football and basketball the reserve clause is somewhat modified, allowing an athlete to "play out his option." After playing for a certain prescribed length of time after he has announced his intentions, at an automatically reduced salary, the player becomes a *free agent*, allowed to offer his services to the highest bidder. However, the modified reserve system of professional football and basketball is accompanied by an *indemnity system* which requires that the club losing the services of a player, who has played out his option, be compensated by the next club with whom that player contracts. In effect, this reduces the player's value to any prospective employer and thus limits his bargaining power in much the same way as does the reserve clause itself. In practice, the exercise of the option is comparatively rare among both football and basketball players.

The reserve rule was instituted in baseball in 1880 to prevent a practice known as "revolving," whereby a player would jump from club to club in response to higher salary offers. Club owners claimed then, as they do today, that such actions would ultimately destroy professional sports.[42] Their arguments are based on three logically distinct premises. First, there is the assertion that the integrity of the game would be threatened if players were allowed to negotiate with clubs other than the one by which they were currently employed. It is felt that an athlete playing against his prospective future employer may not have sufficient incentive to win. Secondly, there is the need for "player continuity and consumer identification" which presumably has a favorable effect on the demand for the product. Finally, and most importantly, it is claimed that without the reserve rule the rich clubs, those located in the superior markets, would bid playing talent away from the clubs in poorer markets, thus monopolizing playing talent and ultimately destroying the industry's product. Economic competition and sporting competition, it is argued, are incompatible given the nature of this product. Such a line of reasoning is filled with implications and assumptions and will be analyzed in greater detail in Chapters 3 and 6.

Whatever the publicly expressed objectives of the reserve rule, there is little doubt that one of its effects is to lower player salaries by depriving the player

---

[42] See, for example, the statement of Ford Frick, Commissioner of the American League, in the Hearings [1964], p. 35, or the statement by Walter Kennedy, Commissioner of the NBA, p. 53, in the same volume.

of the power to bargain in a competitive market for his services.[43] Thus, players' associations, where they exist, are universally opposed to the present structure of the reserve system.[44] With the support of the Major League Baseball Players Association, Curt Flood, an outfielder for the St. Louis Cardinals, and later for the Washington Senators, recently challenged the legality of the reserve clause. The Supreme Court ruled against Flood but, in its decision, indicated that the ultimate resolution of the controversy would require legislative clarification of the position of professional sports relative to the antitrust laws.

In general, the Players Association has urged, not the total abolition of the reserve system, but a modification of it.[45] Some of the suggested amendments to the reserve rule include a temporal limit on the club's option on a player's services, a player's right to "play out his option," and arbitration of salary disputes.

In addition to the reserve rule, the clubs also participate in a *free agent draft*. Free agents, mostly recent high school or college graduates, are those players about to enter the market for playing talent but not yet under contract to any club. Each club chooses, or "drafts," from this pool of talent and thereby acquires the exclusive rights to bargain with those players it has drafted. With respect to player bonuses, the results are analogous to the reserve rule's effect on player salaries: The player's position is such that he is forced to bargain with a potentially discriminatory monopsonist.[46]

The club owners have structured the draft in such a way that the clubs choose in inverse order of their finish, thus strengthening the weaker clubs and penalizing the stronger ones. The ostensible purpose of the draft, therefore, is to promote competitive equality among the members of the league. Due to the club's ability to sell or trade its draft rights, there is some doubt as to the effectiveness of this mechanism. In the NHL's 1971 universal amateur draft, for example, the Montreal Canadiens and the Boston Bruins, the strongest teams in the league, had five of the fourteen first round draft choices between them. They had acquired three of those choices from the weakest teams in the NHL.[47] This and other weaknesses of the draft system are discussed in greater detail in Chapter 3.

---

[43] AFL Commissioner Joe Foss estimates that prior to the merger of the AFL and NFL, the result of their economic competition was an average $2500 increase in the average professional football player's salary. See the Hearings [1964], p. 96.

[44] This has not always been the case. Only recently have players in any sport engaged in anything more than token collective activity. See Flood [1971], Chapter 10, "Discord Backstage," for an account of the history of players organizations in major league baseball.

[45] For the entire text of the players' proposal, see Flood [1971], p. 144.

[46] During the AFL-NFL bidding wars prior to their merger in 1967, free agents' bonuses frequently approached a half-million dollars and more. The present ABA-NBA bidding wars have driven bonuses for many college stars over the million dollar mark and some have reportedly reached $2 million or more.

[47] Leo Monahan, "The Rich Get Richer," THE SPORTING NEWS, June 19, 1971, p. 53. See also the editorial, "A Blessing for the Rich," in the same issue. p. 15.

When a club decides to release a player from his contract he does not necessarily become a free agent. Rather he is put on *waivers* whereby each club in the league, again in inverse order, is given the chance to purchase his contract at a nominal waiver price. If he is "waived through the league," that is, if all teams in the league decline to purchase his contract, he then becomes a free agent. However, if his contract is purchased by a club, he is bound to play for that club.

The Supply of Athletic Talent

The supply of new, trained athletic talent for professional sports flows from two primary sources: minor league farm systems and the colleges. Baseball and hockey rely primarily upon their farm systems, while football and basketball obtain their playing talent almost exclusively from the colleges. The particular source of supply available to a club determines who pays for the athlete's training. In general, a club which relies on a farm system for its players must itself incur the cost of training, while those relying upon colleges reap the financial benefits of college athletic programs.

A club's farm system usually includes ownership of one or more minor league clubs, and so called *working agreements* with others. A working agreement allows the major league club to use the minor league club's facilities as a source of training and developing playing talent and to select specified players from the latter's roster. In return the major league club provides financial assistance, primarily in areas relating to player salaries.

Hockey's farm arrangements are probably the most complex and structured of any sport, covering not only relations between major league (NHL) clubs and minor league clubs, but also their mutual relations with amateur hockey.[48] The NHL controls virtually all organized hockey in Canada to the extent that this segment of the professional sports industry is vertically integrated from top to bottom. Even schoolboy amateurs become bound to a professional club by the time they are sixteen years of age.

Baseball's farm system has declined considerably in the past two decades. In 1949 there were 446 minor league clubs in some 59 leagues. By 1972 the figures had shrunk to 148 clubs in 19 leagues. According to Veeck ([1965], p. 145), television probably accounts as much as anything else for this decline; but many minor league owners claim that the major-minor working agreements, allowing the major league clubs to in effect "raid" the rosters of their minor league affiliates, are the real causes. As Leslie M. O'Connor, former president of the Pacific Coast League, has stated, ". . . practically all Minors came under the Major's thumb. In short they were forced to help build the Majors' player

---

[48] For a detailed analysis of this structure see Jones [1969], p. 145.

monopoly which contributed to their destruction as independent operators. . . ."[49]

With the decline of the minor leagues and the implementation of its own free agent draft in 1965, major league baseball has been turning more toward the colleges as a source of talent. Though they are not as free in their dealings with the colleges as with minor league clubs, the "free" training received in college athletic programs at least partially compensates the clubs for this. On balance, however, when compared with football and basketball, baseball gets relatively few of its players directly from the colleges, and those that it does obtain in the free agent draft are almost always assigned to one of the club's farm teams for further minor league experience.

The fact that most professional football and basketball players come directly from college to the major league club via the free agent draft implies large savings in training costs for these sports vis-à-vis baseball and hockey. The placement burden of training costs, as we shall see, has important implications for the necessity and effectiveness of the labor market restrictions discussed above.

---

[49]Hearings [1964], p. 361.

3

Club Incentives, Collective Action and the Allocation of Playing Talent

As Chapter 2 indicated, the nature of the product and of the production process in the professional team sports industry have important implications for both the individual and joint behavior of clubs within a league. We also suggested that, given the absence of any well developed system of side payments, it is more useful to regard the league organization as an agent for collective choice rather than as a perfect cartel, since collective decision rules, and not centralized authority, are used to reach joint decisions.

In this chapter we analyze individual (and joint) incentives and their implications for the distribution of athletic talent, and hence of relative sporting quality, among the clubs in a league. In addition, we critically examine some of the arguments regarding the effects of, and the necessity for, various institutional constraints on the mobility and distribution of this input.

Individual Club Incentives and Their Implications

There are two plausible specifications of the individual club's objective function. It may act either as a profit maximizer within a given institutional and technological framework, or it may endeavor to maximize an objective function whose arguments include both profit and team quality, or "winning."

Most observers consider the former to be the appropriate working hypothesis. Jones [1969] has shown that profit maximization is entirely consistent with the behavior of the clubs in the National Hockey League, and regarding major league baseball, Koppet ([1967], p. 217) has commented that "when a clear cut choice arises between more victories and more profit, the path toward more profit is chosen."

Accordingly, we accept, as these and other researchers in this field have, the assumption of profit maximization. The utility maximization hypothesis with "winning" as an argument in the utility function would, however, strengthen rather than contradict the conclusions of this chapter, since a club's profits and the quality of its athletic team seem to be positively related over a broad range of observations. If this is true, and if both profits and winning enter positively in the objective function, the maximization of such a function would have the same behavioral implications as would profit maximization alone. The club will benefit by fielding a winning team, via either the utility that the club owners derive from winning, or through the profits that winning generates.

25

There are many ways by which to measure the relative quality of the teams in professional sports. For example, a team that is victorious in at least 50 percent of its games is a "winner." So, in a different sense, is a team which finishes in first place in its league or its division. For his purposes Jones [1969] defines a winning National Hockey League team as one which makes the Stanley Cup playoffs. Still another indicator, and probably the most useful for our purposes, is the measure commonly referred to as "games behind the leader," or *GBL*, which indicates the relative position of a team within its league more accurately than does either rank order or winning percentage.[1] Since we are talking about team quality relative to other teams in the league, this is not a decision variable in the usual sense. Although the *absolute* level of sporting quality of its team can be controlled by the club, *relative* quality, the extent to which the team is a winner or potential winner, is simultaneously determined by the input decisions of all clubs in the league.

A strong positive relation between relative team quality and club profits has often been noted.[2] If, as suggested in Chapter 2, potential consumers derive utility from association with a winning team, then a priori, one would expect that the demand for in-person attendance at games would increase with increases in relative team quality. Even the most casual perusal of attendance data supports this contention. Furthermore, since the potential audience for game broadcasts is also larger for a winning team, it follows that the media's demand for radio and television broadcast rights would also shift upward as team quality improved.

There is yet another revenue source available exclusively to clubs fielding winning teams, and that is *playoff money*. All professional sports leagues are divided into two or more subleagues or "divisions," and at the conclusion of the regular schedule, the first place (and sometimes second or even third place) teams in each division meet in a series of championship playoff games such as the World Series in baseball or the Stanley Cup playoffs in hockey. Each club participating in these playoffs receives a substantial share of the ticket and broadcast revenues which they generate. The size of each participant's share depends in turn upon its finish within the playoffs. The considerable magnitude

---

[1] *GBL* is calculated as follows: Let w_i and l_i be respectively the number of wins and losses by the i-th place team in the league standings. Then GBL_i is given by $1/2[(w_1 - w_i) + (l_i - l_1)]$, where w_1 and l_1 are the number of wins and losses by the league leader. By definition, of course, $GBL_1 = 0$.

A team in second place winning 60 percent of its games, for example, might be only 1/2 game behind the leader, or it might be 10 or more games behind. The two situations are quite different, and this difference is reflected only by the *GBL* measure, not by rank order or winning percentage.

[2] See, for example, Jones ([1969], p. 16) and Koppet ([1967], p. 217). The magnitude of the effect of team quality on the demand for tickets will be explored in depth in Chapter 5.

of this source of revenue provides a powerful incentive for a team to finish high in its division standings.[3]

Though, on the cost side, it is clear that a winning team is not a free good, the available evidence does seem to indicate that, given some suitable operational definition of relative team quality, the latter is closely related to profits. We indicated in Chapter 2 that Davenport [1969] calculated profit rates for the Baltimore Orioles baseball club for the years 1963 through 1966. His calculations, as well as the team's rank finish and GBL in those years are as follows:

Year	Rank Finish	GBL	Rate of Return
1963	4	18-1/2	10.3%
1964	3	2	25.1%
1965	3	8	11.1%
1966	1	0	25.5%

These figures are quite consistent with the assertion of a positive relationship between quality and profits.

As another source of evidence we turn to the data provided in the Hearings [1957] on the financial operations of major league baseball clubs for the years 1952-1956. Defining a winning team as one which finishes in the top half of its eight team division, we can compare its average yearly income, operating expenses, and net revenue with those magnitudes for a losing team over the same period. The results are as follows:

	Winning Team	Losing Team
Revenues	$2,884,000	$1,783,000
Pretax Expenses	2,340,000	1,734,000
Pretax Net Income	$ 544,000	$ 49,000

Nothing has been said yet concerning the range of team quality over which it has a positive effect on club profits. Consideration of this point requires an operational definition of the "range of quality." In a static sense, one could measure a team's relative quality as the probability of its winning any given match or set of matches, thereby restricting the range of quality to the closed, unit interval. In a more dynamic sense, the quality range might be indicated by some measure of a club's dominance over time.

With respect to the static measure, one can ask the question, "Is there a limit to how good a given team can become without adversely affecting its profitabil-

---

[3]For example, playoff and World Series receipts comprised about 14 percent of the total operating income of the Baltimore Orioles baseball club in 1971. See Lester Smith, "Playoff, Series Revenues Put O's Black in '71," THE SPORTING NEWS, April 15, 1972, p. 9.

ity by destroying the contest, or uncertainty, aspect of the product?" Although a complete answer requires a more formal analysis, some casual empiricism suggests that, at least on the revenue side, the limit, if it exists at all, is beyond the range of observable data. Without exception the popularly acknowledged "super teams" appear to have had substantial economic success.

Few teams have ever dominated a professional sport for one season as did the Milwaukee Bucks of the NBA in 1970-71. Winning over 80 percent of all their games and over 90 percent of their home games, average attendance was 98 percent of seating capacity. The previous year, less impressive but still with a winning record and nearly the same personnel, they played to about 80 percent of capacity. Noll and Okner ([1971], p. 16) report that the Buck's gross revenues were nearly one million dollars greater, and their net revenue over $400,000 greater, in the 1970-71 season than in the 1969-70 season.

Nearly as dominant were the 1969-70 New York Knickerbockers, at one point winning 18 consecutive NBA games. Their average attendance was 95 percent of capacity despite the highest ticket prices and the largest arena in the NBA.

If dominance in a sport is measured in dynamic terms, one can observe the apparent economic success of the so-called sports dynasty. The classic case is that of the postwar New York Yankees who won 14 American League pennants between 1949 and 1964. In that 16 year span they led the AL in home attendance 14 times and in road attendance every year.[4] The latter figure actually increased as the period of dominance was extended. The Yankees have not once led the American League in attendance, either home or road, since the quality of the team began to deteriorate in 1965. In addition, as shown in Table 2-2, the market value of the Yankee franchise increased at an average rate of 21 percent per year while the club was a winner, but only by about 2-1/2 percent per year since 1964.

A similar pattern can be observed for the Boston Celtics of the NBA, who dominated that league from 1956 through 1969 winning eleven of thirteen championships. In hockey, the Montreal Canadiens and the Toronto Maple Leafs have between them won 21 of the last 27 Stanley Cup championships, and, as noted in Chapter 2, neither team has played to less than 100 percent of capacity since the war.

Of course, increases in the relative quality of a better than average team will reduce the degree of competitive equality within the league, and if indeed this is a parameter of product quality, the demand functions for all clubs will, other things equal, shift downward. The total effect will however be largely external to

---

[4] According to the Hearings [1957] they also had the highest net income in the American League in every year from 1952 through 1956, except 1954, the only year during that period that they *didn't* win the pennant. In that year the league champion, Cleveland, earned the highest net income among AL clubs. Unfortunately, figures are not available for other years of the Yankee dynasty.

the club which precipitated it, and the effect of decreased competitive equality on its own demand will likely be insignificant in comparison to the benefits derived from winning.

The situation is analogous to the traditional production externality problem. The improvement of a better than average team results in diseconomies which are external to the club in question but internal to the league. Likewise, the improvement of a poor team results in benefits to the league as a whole over and above those which accrue to that individual club.[5] It cannot be expected that the club will consider these external effects of its decisions in determining the level of its team's quality.

In arguing the contrary point, that the preservation of competitive equality is in the interest of the individual club, Rottenberg ([1956], p. 254) contends that though clubs will prefer winning to losing, "they will prefer winning by close margins to winning by wide ones." In an a posteriori sense, this *may* be true. The best of all possible worlds for a club may be to win the championship by the closest possible margin. However, in an uncertain world, the club faces obvious a priori risks of not winning in such a situation, and if there is a positive payoff to winning, such as playoff money, the maximization of expected profits will require winning by more than a close margin.

We conclude, therefore, that the profit maximizing club will have a preference for winning, and not necessarily for winning by a close margin. But by the very definition of "relative quality," some clubs must be frustrated in their desire to field a winning team. Unless the actual distribution of playing talent is one of equality, there must be both winning teams and losing teams, and hence, both more profitable clubs and less profitable clubs.

Of major import for our analysis is the question of how this incentive to win affects the actual distribution of sporting quality, and hence of profits, among the clubs in a league. Let us assume, quite contrary to reality, that there are no restrictions on the markets for quality determining inputs: athletic talent, coaching, and so forth. Let us also assume that the clubs are profit maximizers and, initially, that all clubs in the league operate along identical profit functions.[6] A priori we would expect that the long run interclub distribution of athletic talent would be one of approximate equality. This might mean that in an n-team league each club has a prior probability equal to $1/n$ of winning the championship. Alternatively, we might interpret equality to imply that each team wins exactly 50 percent of its games, each pennant race thus ending in a tie among all n clubs in the league. A third interpretation would have each club finish in first place once every n years.

---

[5] This is true given our implicitly maintained hypothesis that closeness of competition is a parameter of product quality, i.e., that there are positive returns to all clubs from a close pennant race.

[6] It is not necessary to assume strictly identical profit functions, but only that one club's profits, as a function of some quality index, be no more than a vertical displacement of any other club's analogous function.

Of course, even if, as is highly unlikely, the assumption of identical profit functions is met, one would not expect perfect equality, for in reality relative quality is a stochastically determined random variable, subject to outside shocks of relatively large magnitude. The above specifications are meant only to describe the absence of long run, systematic deviations from an equal distribution of playing talent. This is the essence of competitive equality.

The following, highly simplified graphical analysis, may serve to illustrate our point. Suppose that all clubs face identical, strictly concave profit functions, and that profits depend on the quality of the team relative to the rest of the league. This relative team quality depends in turn upon the amount of playing talent employed by the club vis-à-vis the rest of the league. The profit function for any club can therefore be written as $\pi(\ t,\ t^*-t\ )$, where t^* is the total (fixed) supply of athletic talent available to the league, and t is the amount employed by that particular club.

By our assumption of a concave profit function, it follows that marginal profits, π', must be a decreasing function of t. This marginal profits curve is shown in Figure 3-1 labelled π'.

Suppose that playing talent is initially distributed equally within the league so

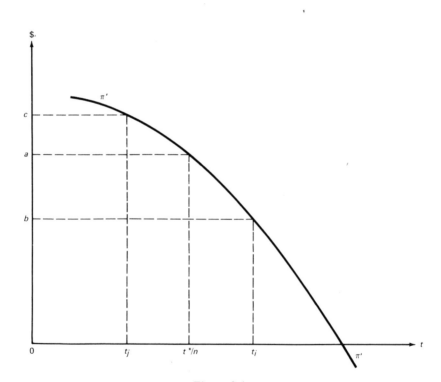

Figure 3-1.

that each club employs t^*/n units of talent. Now assume that some club, say I, increases its share of athletic talent to level t_i. By definition at least one other club, say J, must have its share reduced to a level below t^*/n, for example, to t_j. But this must simultaneously diminish the marginal value of athletic talent to Club I (from a to b) and increase this value for Club J (from a to c). Thus J is now in a position to bid players away from I, and presumably it will continue to do so until the distribution of athletic talent once again reaches t^*/n units for both Club I and Club J. The stable equilibrium is therefore characterized by competitive equality among the clubs in the league.

If now we drop the assumption of identical profit functions, there is no longer any reason to expect a tendency toward long run equality among teams in a league—quite the contrary. We would expect systematic deviations from equality in sporting competition. If, for example, given an initially equal distribution of quality among the teams in a league, the profit functions are such that marginal profit from increased team quality is greater for some clubs than for others, then these former will bid away playing talent from the latter and the result will be a long run tendency for them to field better than average teams. This does not mean that they will always win (or that the other teams will never win), it merely implies long run deviation from equality of competition. The implications for the distribution of profits within the league follow immediately.

Collective Decision and the Allocation
of Athletic Talent

The existence of a severe and prolonged imbalance among teams could conceivably threaten the stability of the league by destroying an essential aspect of the product (uncertainty of outcome), and by creating sporting and financial losers among member clubs. Though some observers, among them Rottenberg [1956], seem to feel that this state of affairs is precluded by the assumption of rational self-interest on the part of all clubs, such is not necessarily the case. If a club finds itself in a situation where its own potential return from fielding a winning team exceeds its potential losses due to a decline in uncertainty of outcome—a distinct possibility in either the short run or the long run—rational behavior would dictate an expansion of its stock of playing talent, even if one of the side effects is decreased competitive equality within the league. Most of the costs of such a policy are external, borne mainly by those other clubs whose relative quality is implicitly decreased.

Though the existence of externalities is neither necessary nor sufficient to warrant the collectivization of an activity, the latter course is likely to evolve whenever the costs of independent action are large relative to the costs imposed by social interdependence.[7] In professional sports the league provides a ready

---

[7]For a comprehensive statement of this, see Buchanan and Tullock [1962], Chapter 5.

vehicle for collective action, including the potential to reallocate playing talent among its members.[8]

Given the legal environment, however, in which the clubs operate and the consequent implications for the potential cost of developing and enforcing an efficient, comprehensive system of side payments, complete collusion is not likely. This in turn rules against the likelihood of joint profit maximization by a profit-sharing cartel among the clubs. Rather, as a true collective body within which individual conflicts are resolved by the application of established decision rules, it is more accurate to speak of the league's *viability* than of its profitability.[9] The implication is that each club receives at least a normal return, while some clubs, presumably those located in superior markets, will receive, in addition, monopoly rents on their territorial rights.[10]

However, the very existence of significant market differences, coupled with positive returns to winning, may make collective reallocation of playing talent improbable and result in a search for alternative joint solutions. The redistributive policies will, by the implications of our argument, be resisted by those clubs in the superior markets, on whom they would impose a net cost.[11] In other words, the redistribution of playing talent will not be a unanimously acceptable solution within the league, and the rich market clubs may be able to block such a collective policy.

The Reserve Rule and Other Restrictions on the Market for Talent Inputs

The chief means by which the league organization seeks to insure its viability is through the constraints it places upon both the demand side and the supply side of the market for athletic talent. In Chapter 2 we noted the existence of two primary institutions which effectively limit the mobility of this singularly

---

[8]This of course is not the only function of the league. Even if there were no conflicts between joint and individual welfare, the league would still serve to introduce economies of scale in such activities as the coordination of schedules, training and supplying referees and other officials, and so forth. These aspects of the league are discussed in more detail in Chapter 6.

[9]Cf. Jones [1960], p. 2.

[10]Given the existence of uncertainty, the league organization may be thought of as analogous to a minimax agent, or an insurance scheme, whereby the individual club is assured of a certain minimum profitability by virtue of its membership.

[11]There is ample evidence that prosperous clubs have in the past resisted attempts to reallocate playing talent. According to Jones ([1969], p. 9), perennial NHL champion Montreal opposed league attempts, in 1954, to institute a draft which would have decreased the effectiveness of its (Montreal's) farm system. According to a recent editorial in THE SPORTING NEWS (June 19, 1971, p. 15), the rich and powerful members of the NHL have acted in such a way as to perpetuate the inferior quality of the expansion clubs and have resisted attempts to reallocate talent to them.

important input, namely, the *reserve clause* in a player's contract and the *free agent draft*.

The nominal purpose of each of these, according to the club owners, is to insure that athletic talent does not become concentrated on one or a few clubs, thereby destroying the profit potential of other clubs and thus the viability of the league. If the market were not so regulated, they contend, the clubs located in the superior markets would simply purchase the services of enough athletic talent to insure that they are perennial (potential) winners. The clubs located in inferior markets would, by implication, become persistent losers and as a result, find their profit potential withering. This is the main argument made by the club owners in their attempts to justify the institutions in question. As our previous analysis has shown, there may be some truth to it. However, before we analyze that argument in detail, let us look at the implications of these institutions for price formation in the markets for athletic talent.

The reserve rule effectively eliminates competitive bidding for the services of a player, and establishes the club which owns his contract as a potential perfectly discriminatory monopsonist with respect to his services.[12] As a highly specialized factor of production whose skills are in short supply, the typical major league player's marginal revenue product in professional sports[13] will exceed that in alternative occupations. The difference between this marginal product and his reservation price (opportunity cost adjusted for psychic satisfaction and the like) is the economic rent accruing to the services of the player. His wage will be determined by a bargaining process with the club and will fall somewhere between his reservation price and his (expected) marginal revenue product to the club. Though the actual price within this range is likely to be indeterminate, further analysis enables us to narrow the range in some realistic cases.

At one extreme, if the player in question is of superior ability, if he is one for which there are few if any substitutes, then he is essentially a monopoly supplier of a very scarce skill. Thus, in this case we have the classic situation of bilateral monopoly, wherein the outcome of the bargaining process is economically indeterminate,[14] depending upon the bargaining skills and other characteristics of the parties involved.[15] There is no reason to expect that the wage will be bid

---

[12] This is strictly true only when there is one league competing for his services. It is not true when there is interleague economic competition as exists now between the ABA and the NBA, or between the NHL and the WHA, or existed prior to the AFL-NFL merger.

[13] This measures the player's capacity to increase the club's revenues both by directly enhancing the entertainment value of the match and through his contribution to the relative quality of the club within its league.

[14] See, for example, Ferguson ([1972], pp. 313-15) for a discussion of indeterminacy in a bilateral monopoly situation.

[15] A recent trend in professional sports has many of the better players conducting their bargaining through specialized agents, presumably to alter the bargaining outcome in the player's favor.

down to the player's reservation price. On the contrary, the more popular the player is, and the higher the level of his athletic skill, the closer should his wage approach his marginal revenue product.[16]

At the other extreme are players of average ability for whom there are many good substitutes. Here we have the case of a market which is competitive on the seller's side and monopsonistic on the buyer's side, with the buyer in fact a potential price discriminator. Still we should not necessarily expect the wage to fall to the player's reservation price. In baseball and hockey (and to a lesser extent in football and basketball) the club provides training for players, and the institutions in question insure that this training is specific to the club with whom the player has contracted. As Becker ([1964], pp. 21-22) has argued, if there is any possibility of labor turnover, the wage of a specifically trained employee will be above his alternate marginal product. This, along with the above bilateral monopoly case, helps to explain why the reported average salary of major league athletes seems to exceed their likely alternative earnings.[17]

In cases where the clubs provide training we would also have to revise our upper limit on players' salaries. As Becker ([1964], p. 28) has shown, under these conditions the employee's wage will be less than his marginal product by an amount sufficient to yield a return on the training provided by the firm.

We can expect, therefore, that a player's salary will lie somewhere within a range whose lower bound is slightly higher than his reservation price, and whose upper bound is lower than his marginal revenue product by an amount sufficient to yield the club an acceptable return on its investment in his training.

On the other hand, if the market for players' services were allowed to function unhindered by the institutions under consideration, we would expect three things: First, most training would become general rather than specific and as such the burden of training would fall elsewhere than on the clubs. This does not necessarily imply that it would be shifted entirely to the players. At present the major costs of training professional football and basketball players, for example, are borne neither by the players nor by the clubs, but by colleges and universities engaged in intercollegiate athletic competition in these sports.[18] (As indicated in Chapter 2, the same is only partially the case in baseball and hockey.)

---

[16] Noll and Okner ([1971], p. 50) seem to feel that the salaries of some NBA "superstars" in fact approach quite closely their contribution to the club's revenue. It should be noted, however, that their observations cover a period of competitive bidding between NBA and ABA clubs.

[17] In 1968 for example, the average major league baseball player's salary was 50 percent higher than that of a family whose head had received four or more years of college education. The latter, according to THE HANDBOOK OF LABOR STATISTICS 1970, was $15,704. The average player's salary was $22,000 in 1966 and had risen to $37,000 by 1973. It is worth noting, however, that these salary means are inflated by the very high salaries of a relatively few "superstars." Flood ([1971], p. 136) contends that the *median* salary in major league baseball in 1969 was less than $20,000, and that 18 percent of the players received the $10,000 minimum. The median salary in 1973 is $31,000.

[18] See, for example, Koch [1971].

Secondly, a player's salary would be bid up to his marginal revenue product where he, rather than the club, would reap both the economic rent resulting from his natural talent and the return to his share of the investment in his training.

Finally, playing talent would be allocated in such a way that the marginal revenue product of this input would be equal for all clubs. This equality at the margin does not, as we have argued, imply an equal distribution of playing talent among the teams in a league. On the contrary, such a distribution would occur only in a special case, the general rule being a nonequal distribution of playing talent among the clubs. It is for this reason that the club owners claim the need for the reserve rule, the free agent draft, and other restrictions on the mobility of players. They claim that without these institutions the viability of the league organization would be threatened.

Though we cannot agree with the entire argument as usually stated, it does contain some elements of truth. In particular we agree that, given existing institutional arrangements in professional sports, without some joint action on the part of the clubs, the distribution of playing talent among them will not be equal. However, the significance of this conclusion rests on the nature of the market differences contributing to the skewness of the distribution. If the relevant differences are significant, exogenous and persistent in the long run, they may indeed threaten the viability of a league, at least as presently constituted. A list of intermarket characteristics which potentially fall into this category would include such variables as population and the availability of substitutes in the form of alternate sources of entertainment.

If, however, the relevant market differences are insignificant or of a basically unstable, short run nature, joint action on the part of league members may not be necessary. For example, if cyclical interregional income differentials have a significant effect on the distribution of playing talent, the effects would be temporary and would not necessarily threaten the league's viability.[19] The same would be true if the quality differences result from variations in management acumen.[20]

Let us assume for the present that long run intermarket differences do exert a significant effect upon individual team quality via their effects on the profit functions of the respective clubs. Can we conclude, then, that the present collective institutions designed ostensibly to promote sporting competition are justified or even effective? The answer on both counts is, "No." Certain aspects of the present reserve system and free agent draft rules suggest that their actual effects with respect to the distribution of athletic quality are likely to be quite insignificant.

---

[19] Of course, if recurring cyclical downswings *always* struck a given market or set of markets more intensively than others, this disturbance could be considered long run rather than short run.

[20] The decline of the New York Yankees since 1965 has often been attributed to poor management within that organization. See, for example, Jim Ogle, "Gibbs Case Pinpoints Yankee Failure to Rebuild," THE SPORTING NEWS, July 10, 1971, p. 3.

Characteristic of each of the four sports under study are well developed and highly organized markets within which the clubs engage in the exchange of player contracts and of rights to draft free agents. The player's contract, as an exclusive option on his services, is a marketable commodity as are the draft rights enabling a club to bargain exclusively with a free agent. If the clubs are profit maximizers, these aspects of the talent input market would have the effect of distributing playing talent in nearly the same manner as would competitive markets.[21] If a player's marginal revenue product is higher with another club than with the club which presently owns his contract, it will be profitable to sell his contract at a price somewhere between the present values of the two alternate productivities. Playing talent will be allocated to those clubs whose marginal profit from increased quality is greater, and market equilibrium will be characterized by equality at the margin rather than by equal average qualities among the clubs. The only difference between this allocation and that which would result from competitive labor markets is that the latter may reflect player preferences among various markets on the basis of location, climate, or other factors. A priori, however, the two distributions would be quite similar.

Much of the available evidence is consistent with the contention that the present structure of the labor market institutions does *not* necessarily lead to long run equality in the distribution of talent. In major league baseball, which instituted the reserve rule in 1880, the New York Yankees won 29 of 50 American League championships between 1920 and 1970, while during that same period the Boston Red Sox won two pennants and the Chicago White Sox but one. In the National League, between 1920 and 1957, New York, Brooklyn, and St. Louis had won 26 of 38 league championships among them, while Philadelphia and Pittsburgh had each won only once.

In professional football, New York and Cleveland won 17 of 21 NFL Eastern Conference titles between 1949 and 1969. Neither Pittsburgh in the Eastern Conference, nor San Francisco in the Western Conference had ever won a divisional championship.

In hockey the distribution of playing talent has been even more skewed. Twenty-two of the last 30 Stanley Cups have been won by either Toronto or Montreal, while New York has won only one Cup in the past 40 years.

An analysis of the free agent draft reveals similar ineffectiveness in this area. The draft is structured in such a way that the teams draft in inverse order of their most recent league rank, and it may thus be interpreted as an attempt to redistribute athletic talent. In general, however, the inverse draft can be expected to be relatively ineffective in accomplishing this goal. This point has been argued rather convincingly by Koppet [1972]. Let us assume a league of twenty teams and a five round player draft. The club which finished the season in last place will thus have selections 1, 21, 41, 61, and 81 in the draft, while the first place finisher will have selections 20, 40, 60, 80, and 100. Clearly, the only

---

[21] Rottenberg ([1956], p. 254) makes the same point.

real difference is a single player, the first choice in the draft, and this difference becomes even less if we are considering the opportunity for mediocre (rather than last place) clubs in attaining parity with the better clubs via the inverse draft.

In addition, since collegiate accolades or other past performance indicators are rather imperfect predictors of future potential, an extensive scouting system is at least as important as a club's relative position in the player draft.

Finally, the club's ability to sell or trade its draft rights can also defeat any effects the draft might have as an agent for promoting competitive equality.

A most striking recent example, the 1971 National Hockey League draft, illustrates the potential weaknesses in the free agent draft as a force for equalization of playing strength among members of a league. Among them, the three worst clubs in the NHL had no first round selections at all, having dealt these away to three of the most powerful and successful clubs. The Los Angeles Kings have in fact traded away all of their first round draft picks until 1975, and all they had to show for this in 1971 was the next to worst record in the NHL. On the other hand the Montreal Canadiens, perennial champions and 1971 Stanley Cup winners, had three first round choices in 1971, four in 1972, and three more in 1973.

According to *The Sporting News*, " . . . the old line clubs made certain that draft rights would be as conveyable as General Motors stock certificates. When expansion clubs tried to dicker with the old franchises for something better than the castoffs they got in the beginning, they usually found they could do business only with draft rights. Under those conditions the strong entries did not require genius leadership to remain strong."[22]

An implication of our analysis is that the distribution of profits within the league should therefore also be skewed. Noll and Okner ([1971], pp. 19-31) argue that this is in fact the case in the National Basketball Association, where the league as a whole is profitable, but where profits are highly concentrated in the New York, Los Angeles, and Milwaukee franchises. The other franchises are either earning close to normal returns, they assert, or are suffering losses.

If, as the owners claim, the purpose of the reserve clause and the free agent draft is to prevent one club, or a small set of clubs, from dominating a particular sport, we can only conclude that they have failed miserably. The fact that players' contracts and future draft selections are marketable commodities assures the impotence of these institutions in significantly altering the competitive market distribution of playing talent. In fact the stronger clubs usually resist any genuine attempts to establish competitive equality for, as our previous analysis has indicated, the individual profit maximizing club is likely to find winning preferable to increased balance within the league.

As other writers have suggested, a very simple way to achieve competitive

---

[22]"A Blessing for the Rich," THE SPORTING NEWS, June 19, 1971. See also the column by Leo Monahan, "The Rich Get Richer," on p. 53 of the same issue.

equality might be to allow weaker clubs to periodically draft some specified number of players from stronger clubs.[23] The stronger clubs have always resisted schemes such as this.

Why then do these constraints on labor mobility continue to exist? The answer, to which we have already alluded, is quite straightforward. The reserve clause and the free agent draft insure the viability of the league not through their effect on the interclub distribution of playing talent, but by lowering the cost curves of *all* clubs in the league sufficiently to insure the economic survival of even the perennial losers. The economic rent which, in a competitive market, would accrue to the player as a specialized factor of production, is usurped by the club which owns his contract, or the draft rights to him if he is a free agent.

Curt Flood ([1971, pp. 138-39), the former major league baseball player who lost his suit against organized baseball, makes this point quite lucidly:

According to this (the club owners') pessimistic theory, if baseball players were as free to shop for employment as actors are, the richest club would hire all the stars, making a shambles of every pennant race. The implication is that some teams are too poor to compete for talent in the open market. The present reserve system protects them from that catastrophe. Reduced to its essentials, the argument suggests that baseball players now subsidize their employers by working at cut rates.

. . . No major-league baseball corporation is presently in financial straits. If any were, it seems to me that subsidies should come not from the employees but from the suffering owner's fellow monopolists. . . . Unless I misread history, we have passed the stage when indentured servitude was justifiable on the grounds that the employer could not afford the cost of normal labor.

Even in professional football and basketball where a nominal limit is placed on the temporal length of the club's exclusive option on a player's services, the situation is not much different. It is a rare occurrence for a player to "play out his option," mainly because this action is discouraged by the costs imposed on any player choosing to do so. A player wishing to terminate his contract with a club and become a free agent must make a prior announcement of this intention, usually one year in advance. In the interim he must accept an automatic 20 percent (NFL) or 25 percent (NBA) cut in salary. During the course of his "lame duck" year he faces the risk of a poor athletic performance, or even injury, which can substantially reduce his bargaining power when his free agent status is established.[24] In addition, when the player finally does become a free agent, it is unlikely that any bid for his services will approach his marginal revenue product, for league rules require that the new employer compensate his former club with one or more players of equivalent worth. This of course reduces his potential value to any prospective bidder.

---

[23] Cf. the statement by Leslie M. O'Connor, in the Hearings [1964], specifically p. 376.

[24] If he were *not* playing out his option and played poorly (or suffered a minor injury), this risk would be minimized, since league rules stipulate that his salary cannot be cut by more than 10 percent from one season to the next (*if* he stays with the same employer).

It has also been charged that the club owners in order to discourage the practice of playing out an option, have resorted at times to formally or informally blackballing players who have engaged in this practice.[25] If in fact this does occur, it should do so with greater frequency among mediocre players where the economic incentives of any club might be outweighed by peer pressure from other clubs. If the player is a star, such a mutual blackballing practice is likely to prove unstable.

Summary and Some Implied Hypotheses

We now summarize the arguments of this chapter and indicate some of the questions and hypotheses implied by our model as developed so far.

First, an apparent conflict exists between the behavior resulting from independent profit maximization by individual clubs and the viability of the league. Individual clubs find a positive return to a winning team; but intermarket differences in these returns, combined with the fact that winning, or relative quality, is a jointly determined aspect of the club's product, guarantee that some clubs will be persistent losers. In markets where the (marginal) returns to winning are higher the incentive to win will be realized; in markets where returns are lower it will be frustrated. Profits will be distributed accordingly among the clubs.

This situation is a threat to the long run viability of the league. But, since the weaker clubs, as well as the stronger ones, have a voice in collective legislation, steps will be taken to preserve the viability of the league.

The most obvious course of action is to redistribute playing talent to insure a more even distribution of quality than would result from unconstrained independent action. The present restrictions on the talent input markets were constructed with this as their nominal goal, but both a priori analysis and the historical record suggest their impotence in this respect. Redistribution is likely to impose costs on the stronger clubs, who would therefore resist such a policy. This is especially true when a well-developed system of side payments is lacking.

A second method of insuring the viability of the league is to lower the costs of all clubs. This, rather than a redistribution of playing talent, has been the major result of the reserve rule and the free agent draft. These institutions have enabled professional sports clubs to usurp much of the economic rent which, under competitive conditions, would accrue to the players themselves.

Formal empirical methods, rather than the casual empiricism presented so far, are necessary to test some of the hypotheses implied by our model. We must investigate the incentives of the individual club with regard to winning vis-à-vis maintaining league balance. Due to lack of hard data concerning costs, we will approach this question mainly from the revenue side within the context of a model of the demand for tickets to professional sporting events.

---

[25] Cf. the interview with Ned Doyle, et al., "Rap," BLACK SPORTS, August, 1971, p. 46.

We then must determine the extent to which intermarket differences, especially long run, exogenous differences, affect the distribution of playing talent among the clubs in a league. If these differences do not exist, or if they are insignificant in comparison with short run random effects on team quality, we must conclude that competitive markets and league viability are not incompatible.

Finally, if collective action is indeed necessary to insure league viability, we must investigate the existence of more equitable and more efficient alternatives to the present reserve system.

It is to these questions that we now turn. In Chapter 4, a more formal model of the determination of optimal team quality is constructed and used to generate some hypotheses concerning the distribution of playing talent. In Chapter 5, empirical tests, including estimation of a demand model, will be conducted. In the light of the resulting conclusions, Chapter 6 analyzes present and potential public policy toward the professional sports industry.

4

A Model of Team Quality Determination

In this chapter we attempt to formalize some of the hypotheses suggested above by deriving the implications of a rather straightforward model of the professional sports firm in its role as an employer of athletic talent. The approach taken is that of comparative statics analysis with little or no explicit consideration of the implied underlying adjustment process.

For our present purposes we accept, as given, certain characteristics of the institutional structure within which the club operates. In particular, we assume that the league association has endowed each club with the "territorial rights" to a given market and with a predetermined schedule setting forth the number and locations of all games, both home and road, in which the club is to participate. Each team is assumed to play every other team in the league twice, once at home and once on the road, and attendance at these games is the sole source of revenue for the club.

The exclusion of broadcast revenues will have no substantive effect on our conclusions if, as we have previously suggested, the variables affecting broadcast demand are the same as those affecting demand for in-person audience. In particular, team quality, market population, and other market parameters should affect the demand for game broadcasts in a manner analogous to the way in which they affect ticket demand. Thus with the number of games fixed by the league's schedule, the main decision variables confronting the club are the quality parameters of its product and the product's price. The club is assumed to control the former via the stock of athletic talent which it employs and to set a single admission price for all of its home games. Since clubs typically engage in multipart pricing with respect to various seating categories, our single price may be interpreted as the weighted average price resulting from an optimal multipart pricing decision on the part of the club.

Each club is assumed to act as a Cournot—independent profit maximizer, isolated by its territorial monopoly from direct price competition from other league members, and determining its optimal stock of athletic talent based upon the given quality of all other clubs in the league.[1] Here, the appropriateness of the Cournot postulate seems open to less criticism than it usually attracts in other applications. There is, in fact, some evidence to suggest that the managements of professional sports clubs, as well as most neutral observers, do actually resort to the essentially naive forecasting method implied by the Cournot hypothesis: namely the extension of recent past performance as a

---

[1] The Cournot assumption is also made by El-Hodiri and Quirk [1971], p. 1308.

forecast of future performance.[2] Ultimately, of course, the test of this as well as any other assumptions, lies not in their a priori "reasonableness," but in the predictive power of the model and in the empirical validity of the hypotheses which it generates.[3]

The Demand for the Product

Let us imagine a market populated by n firms, each of which produces a single, differentiated product. If the general relations of complementarity and substitutability hold among the various products, we can write the demand function for the product of the i-th firm as $d_i(p,x)$, where p and x are n-dimensional vectors of prices and product quality indices, respectively. These latter presumably incorporate information about any parameters affecting consumer preferences among the various products. By the conventional definitions[4] the products of two firms, i and j, are classified as gross substitutes if, *ceteris paribus*, $(\partial d_i/\partial p_j) > 0$ and $(\partial d_i/\partial x_j) < 0$, and as gross complements when these inequalities are reversed, for $i \neq j$.

Our concern is with a special case of the above, namely, that in which interfirm effects of product quality variation exist, but where price competition is absent. This is essentially the relation among the clubs in a professional sports league: Each club is established as a territorial monopolist within its own market, but the athletic talent input decision of any one club affects both intraleague competitiveness and relative qualities, and hence affects the product demand of every other league member.

Let us assume an n-club league in which each club's revenues are generated by the sale of tickets to the matches in which it is a participant. Define q^{ij} as the expected number of tickets an average or "representative" consumer in the i-th club's market will purchase to attend that team's game against the j-th team. Each q^{ij} is assumed to be functionally dependent upon the ticket price set by club i, say p_i, and upon the quality parameters of the match between i and j. We have previously enumerated these latter as (1) uncertainty of outcome, (2) entertainment value, and (3) the potential association with a winning team for consumers in the i-th market. Each of these in turn depends upon the absolute

---

[2] Preseason pennant race forecasts almost invariably show extremely high correlation with the final standing of the previous season. For example, in THE SPORTING NEWS of April 10, 1971, there appeared three separate predictions of the outcome of the 1971 major league baseball pennant races: One by THE SPORTING NEWS, one by the Baseball Writers Association of America, and one based upon preseason Las Vegas odds. The rank correlation coefficients of these forecasts with the previous season's finish were respectively, 0.872, 0.900, 0.886. It is interesting to note, in retrospect, that the rank correlation between the 1970 finish and the *actual* 1971 finishes is only 0.403.

[3] See, for example, Friedman [1953].

[4] See, for example, Hicks [1946], pp. 42ff.

quality of both clubs. Thus, measuring the i-th club's quality by some index of the amount of athletic talent that it employs, say x_i, we can write the total seasonal demand for tickets by the individual consumer in this club's market as

$$q^i = q^i(p_i, x, m_i) = \sum_{j \neq i} q^{ij}, \qquad (4\text{-}1)$$

where x is an n-dimensional vector of team qualities, or more specifically athletic talent inputs, such that $x = (x_1, \ldots, x_n)$, and $m_i = (m_{i1}, \ldots, m_{ir})$ is a vector of the relevant characteristics of the i-th club's market, including such things as available entertainment of recreational substitutes, the quality and accessibility of arena or stadium facilities, and possibly sociocultural variables such as the community's ethnic make-up.

Now if the population of the i-th club's market is N_i, the total (seasonal) demand for tickets to the i-th club's home matches is $Q^i = N_i q^i$, and the demand for tickets to the away games played by that club in the markets of the other n — 1 league members is equal to $\sum_{j \neq i} N_j q^{ji}$. We assume further that $\partial Q^i / \partial p_i < 0$ and $\partial Q^i / \partial x_i > 0$ in the range under consideration.

The Club's Cost Function

For our purposes the club's costs can be divided into two categories: those associated with supplying seats at matches, and those incurred in hiring, training, and maintaining athletic talent. It seems reasonable to assume that costs of the first type, call them "game-specific" costs, can be further divided into a fixed and a variable component. There are certain fixed costs of putting on a game such as the costs of opening the arena or stadium, lighting costs, and so forth. In addition, there are costs incurred in the actual supplying of seats to ticket buyers, costs which, we assume, vary proportionately with the number of seats sold.[5] We can therefore write the cost of supplying seats at games, given the schedule determined by the league, as

$$C^{1i} = F_i + h_i Q^i \qquad (4\text{-}2)$$

---

[5] With respect to their purchases of variable inputs, clubs attempt, apparently with a good degree of accuracy, to make prior estimates of game crowds for the purposes of hiring the requisite variable labor input (parking lot attendants, security forces, vendors, etc.). These estimates are based upon the particular opponent, the weather, the day of the week, and so forth.

where C^{1i} are the i-th club's game-specific costs, F_i are total (seasonal) fixed costs of meeting the predetermined schedule, and h_i, the (constant) marginal cost of supplying additional seats.[6] Assume further that $F_i = (n-1)f_i$ where f_i is the fixed cost per game.

Those costs associated with the input of athletic talent, and thus with the i-th team's quality, we will write

$$C^{2i} = G^i(x_i), \qquad (4\text{-}3)$$

where we assume that the marginal cost of athletic talent is a nondecreasing function of x, that is, $\partial^2 G^i/\partial x_i^2 \geqslant 0$.

The club's total costs are therefore given by

$$C^i = C^{1i} + C^{2i} = F_i + h_i Q^i + G^i. \qquad (4\text{-}4)$$

Note that the above formulation implies a distinction between the direct and the indirect cost effects of an increase in the club's utilization of athletic talent. First, there is the direct marginal cost of purchasing talent, $\partial G^i/\partial x_i$. The indirect effect arises because changes in x_i also affect Q^i, and therefore the total marginal cost of a change in x_i is the total derivative of (4-4), namely

$$\frac{dC^i}{dx_i} = h_i Q_i^i + G_i^i \qquad (4\text{-}5)$$

where the i *subscripts* on the functions Q and G indicate partial derivatives taken with respect to x_i.

First Order Conditions for Maximum Profit

In this model, the club's revenues consist of its respective shares of both the home and road proceeds arising from the sale of tickets to games in which it participates. The usual method of determining the visitor's share of the total gate is via the application of some league-determined proportion, say v, to the revenues, net of game specific costs, generated by the sale of tickets for that game.[7] Thus, the total net revenue accruing to the i-th club from its home games and from its road games are given respectively by

---

[6] We have implicitly assumed here that, at least within the relevant range, the capacity constraint is not binding.

[7] As noted previously, the visitor's share may also be determined as a fixed amount per ticket, as among the National League baseball clubs where the visiting team receives 27-1/2 cents per ticket sold.

$$(1 - v)(p_i Q^i - F_i - h_i Q^i) \tag{4-6a}$$

$$v[\ \underset{j \neq i}{\Sigma}\ (p_j N_j q^{ji} - f_j - h_j N_j q^{ji})]. \tag{4-6b}$$

For the profits of the i-th club we may therefore write

$$\pi^i = (1 - v)\ [(p_i - h_i)Q^i - F_i] + v\left\{\ \underset{j \neq i}{\Sigma}\ [N_j q^{ji}(p_j - h_j) - f_j]\ \right\} - G^i(x_i). \tag{4-7}$$

We have assumed that the club acts as a profit maximizing, Cournot-independent agent, whose decision variables are p_i and x_i, and it is thus in equilibrium when the following set of first order conditions are satisfied:[8] $\pi_p^i = 0; \pi_i^i = 0$. (Again the subscripts indicate partial derivatives, p, with respect to price, and i, with respect to x_i.) More specifically these conditions may be written

$$(1 - v)\ [Q^i + (p_i - h_i)Q_p^i]\ = 0 \tag{4-8a}$$

$$(1 - v)(p_i - h_i)Q_i^i + v\underset{j \neq i}{\Sigma} N_j(p_j - h_j)q_i^{ji} - G_i^i = 0. \tag{4-8b}$$

Since $(1 - v) > 0$, (4-8a) implies that $(p_i - h_i) = -Q^i/Q_p^i$ and if all clubs are profit maximizers this must hold for all i. This of course is nothing more than the standard condition for optimal pricing policy,[9] and if it is substituted into (4-8b), a consolidated form of the firm's first order equilibrium condition is readily obtained, namely

$$(1 - v)\frac{p_i Q_i^i}{e_p^i}\ +\ v\left[\underset{j \neq i}{\Sigma} N_j \frac{p_j q_i^{ji}}{e_p^j}\right] - G_i^i\ = 0, \tag{4-9}$$

where $e_p^i = -(p_i/Q^i)Q_p^i$ is the price elasticity of demand for tickets in the i-th club's market. It is defined as a positive number since $Q_p^i < 0$.

Equation (4-9) is the implicit reaction function for the i-th club. Its solution yields the club's optimal input of athletic talent, say x_i^0. The distribution of athletic talent among all the clubs in the league is implied in the simultaneous

---

[8] Second order conditions for a maximum will be discussed below. They are assumed to hold at this point by our previous specification of concave profit functions.

[9] It is a trivial exercise to show that the condition implies the familiar optimal pricing rule; that is, $p = MC[e/(e-1)]$, where e is the direct price elasticity of demand and MC is the marginal cost of supplying output.

solution to a system of the n equations, one for each club, analogous to (4-9). This solution provides us with the vector of optimal team quality, $x^0 = (x_1^0, \ldots, x_n^0)$, in the case of Cournot-independent behavior.

It appears that the club's optimal level of athletic talent depends upon not only the sensitivity of potential consumers to changes in the club's quality (Q_i^i and q^{ji}), and on the marginal cost of athletic talent (G_i^i), but also upon the ordinary demand elasticities in the various markets in which the club performs (e_p^i and e_p^j).[10]

The Role of the Visitor's Gate Share

The jointly optimal distribution of athletic talent among league members will, in general, differ from x^0 described above. This joint profit maximizing solution can easily be shown to be the vector, $x^* = (x_1^*, \ldots, x_n^*)$, which is the solution to the following set of n equations:

$$\frac{p_i Q_i^i}{e_p^i} + \sum_{j \neq i} \frac{p_j Q_i^j}{e_p^j} - G_i^i = 0 \qquad (i = 1, \ldots, n). \qquad (4\text{-}10)$$

Note that, in this solution, all effects of the i-th team's quality are taken into account and given equal weight. At the optimum, each club's marginal talent costs, G_i^i, are balanced against the effect of variations in x_i on that club's demand as well as on the demand functions of all other $n - 1$ clubs in the league. These latter cross effects are not generally taken into full account when the club acts independently, for they are externalities generated by variations in the club's employment of athletic talent.

We may expect that if these externalities impose significant costs on a sufficient number of firms,[11] the league, acting as a collective body, may endeavor to correct the situation by internalizing them to some extent. The establishment of a positive visitor's gate share can be interpreted as a collective mechanism for accomplishing just this, by at least partially internalizing these external effects.

If $v = 0$, that is if there is no visitor's share, then the Cournot-independent equilibrium condition reduces to a special case of (4-9), namely

$$\frac{p_i Q_i^i}{e_p^i} = G_i^i. \qquad (4\text{-}11)$$

---

[10]This is a standard result in a model in which product price and quality are jointly determined. See, for example, Dorfman and Steiner [1954], pp. 832-33.

[11]Just what number of clubs is "sufficient," of course, depends upon the particular decision rule employed by the league in arriving at collective decisions.

In this case, the reaction functions include only the effects of variations in the athletic talent input on the demand for tickets in the club's home market. In general, the optimal stock of athletic talent will be larger (1) the larger the effect of a marginal change in team quality on demand for tickets, (2) the less price-elastic the demand for tickets, and (3) the lower the marginal cost of athletic talent.

An analysis quite similar to this is made by Dorfman and Steiner ([1954], pp. 833ff). They conclude that the wider the variation in factors analogous to (1)-(3) above, *within* a given market, the more broadly differentiated will be the products in that market, and vice versa. Paralleling their argument, we can state that the greater the variation in these factors *among* the various markets, the greater the differences in the optimal stock of athletic talent among the clubs in those markets, and hence the less egalitarian the distribution of relative quality among the clubs. When $v = 0$, the effects of a change in x_i on demand in other markets is given zero weight in the club's decision rule, and thus intermarket differences will exert their maximum effects on the distribution of athletic talent.[12]

Now assuming some nonzero, positive value of v, we can see from equilibrium condition (4-9) that the i-th club must consider the effects of variations in its employment of athletic talent on the demand for tickets in markets other than its own. Specifically, the cross effects, q_i^{ji}, must enter into its profit calculations with respect to x_i^0. The role of the positive visitor's gate share is therefore to partially mitigate effects of intermarket differences by incorporating the cross effects, otherwise external, into the decision function of the individual firm.[13] The extent to which this is accomplished is of course dependent upon the actual value, collectively agreed upon, of the parameter, v. The larger v, the greater the weight placed upon the cross effects relative to the own-market effects of a change in x_i. The value of v implied by the joint optimum conditions (4-10) is $v = 1/2$, but such extreme egalitarianism is not a likely outcome of the collective decision process, given the costs it imposes on clubs in the superior markets. Nor, as will be shown in Chapter 6, is it necessarily the value of v which results in equality within the league, that is, $x_i^0 = x_j^0$ for any i, j. In other words,

---

[12] The existence and direction of the effects of intermarket differences is discussed in more detail below.

[13] It should also be noted that the cross-effect terms in the Cournot-independent model [Equation (4-9)] are not identical to the analogous cross terms in the jointly optimal conditions, (4-10). These intermarket effects differ by an amount equal to

$$\sum_{k \neq i, j} N_j (p_j/e_p^j) q_i^{jk} = (p_j/e_p^j)(Q_i^j - N_j \; q_i^{ji}),$$

which is the effect of variations in x_i on the revenue generated by matches between all *other* teams, j and k. This difference may not be negligible, though a priori we would expect it to be much smaller than the q_i^{ji} terms.

maximum joint profits will not in general imply complete equality of playing strengths among league members.

The Comparative Statics of
Intermarket Differences

We now turn to an investigation of the model's implications concerning the qualitative effects of variations in certain market parameters on the club's optimal employment of athletic talent. Specifically we are interested in the sign of the comparative statics derivative, dx_i^0/dm, where m is some exogenously shifting market parameter affecting any or all of the factors identified above, namely, Q_i^i and q_i^{ij}, e_p^i, or G_i^i.

In order to sign this derivative, it is necessary that we first examine the second order conditions which insure that (4-8a) and (4-8b) describe a maximum rather than a minimum or saddle point. These conditions require that the profit function be concave in both p and x, and, hence, that the following conditions on the second order partials be met:

$$\pi_{pp}^i < 0; \; \pi_{ii}^i < 0; \; \pi_{pp}^i \, \pi_{ii}^i - (\pi_{pi}^i)^2 > 0. \tag{4-12}$$

Sufficient for inequalities (4-12) to hold is that revenues be strictly concave in both p and x, and that marginal costs be nondecreasing in Q and x. We assume that these conditions are met, that is, that Equations (4-8) describe a profit maximum.

In order to obtain unambiguous signs on the required comparative statics derivatives, we must sign the cross partial of the profit function, π_{pi}^i. A sufficient, though *not* a necessary, condition for this cross partial to be unambiguously positive, is that an improvement in the club's quality, other things equal, diminishes the price elasticity of demand for its product.[14] This particular assumption intuitively seems quite palatable, since it corresponds to, among other

---

[14] The proof of this is straightforward: Slightly rewriting condition (4-8a) we obtain

$$\pi_p^i = (1-v)Q^i \left(1 - \frac{p_i - h_i}{p_i} \, e_p^i\right) = 0.$$

Differentiating this with respect to x_i gives

$$\pi_{pi}^i = (1-v)Q^i \left[-\frac{p_i - h_i}{p_i}\right] \frac{\partial e_p^i}{\partial x_i} + (1-v)Q_i^i(1 - \frac{p_i - h_i}{p_i} \, e_p^i).$$

The last term in brackets must be zero by the first order condition above, and the first two factors in the first term on the right are positive, while the third factor must be negative. Hence the sign of π_{pi}^i will be the opposite of the sign of $\partial e_p^i/\partial x_i$.

cases, that in which quality changes induce parallel shifts in the demand curve.[15] We therefore make the assumption that the cross partial of the profit function is positive.

Now if some parameter, m, changes, then both x_i and p_i must be adjusted in such a way as to maintain the first order conditions given in (4-8). This is equivalent to requiring that the total differentials of π_p^i and π_i^i must be zero,[16] or, dropping the i superscripts and subscripts for simplicity:

$$d\pi_p = \pi_{pp}dp^0 + \pi_{pi}dx^0 + \pi_{pm}dm = 0$$

$$d\pi_i = \pi_{ip}dp^0 + \pi_{ii}dx^0 + \pi_{im}dm = 0.$$

The straightforward application of Cramer's rule gives the required comparative statics adjustment derivatives:

$$\frac{dx^0}{dm} = \frac{\pi_{ip}\pi_{pm} - \pi_{pp}\pi_{im}}{\pi_{ii}\pi_{pp} - \pi_{ip}^2} \qquad (4\text{-}13a)$$

$$\frac{dp^0}{dm} = \frac{\pi_{ip}\pi_{im} - \pi_{ii}\pi_{pm}}{\pi_{ii}\pi_{pp} - \pi_{ip}^2} . \qquad (4\text{-}13b)$$

The denominators on the right sides of both of these equations must be positive by the second order conditions, and hence we can state the following sign conditions on the comparative statics derivatives:

$$\operatorname{sgn}\left(\frac{dx^0}{dm}\right) = \operatorname{sgn}\left(\pi_{ip}\pi_{pm} - \pi_{pp}\pi_{im}\right) \qquad (4\text{-}14a)$$

$$\operatorname{sgn}\left(\frac{dp^0}{dm}\right) = \operatorname{sgn}\left(\pi_{ip}\pi_{im} - \pi_{ii}\pi_{pm}\right). \qquad (4\text{-}14b)$$

Our concern here is primarily with the effects of variations in market parameters on team quality, and thus with (4-14a).

Market Population

One of the more important market variables with which we are concerned is the population of the "home" market area in which the club operates. More specifi-

---

[15] Of course we need not assume that demand shifts are parallel, only that either $Q_{ip}^i \geq 0$, or that, if it is negative, it is small in absolute value.

[16] See Samuelson [1947], pp. 12ff.

cally we wish to predict the effects, if any, of intermarket population differences on the clubs' optimal stocks of athletic talent. The sign of the comparative statics deriviative dx_i^0/dN_i, where N_i is the population of the i-th club's market, tells us the direction of this population effect, and in order to sign this derivative, we must be able to first sign the second order cross partials of the profit function with respect to population, namely π_{iN} and π_{pN}, since by (4-14a)

$$\text{sgn}(\frac{dx^0}{dN}) = \text{sgn}(\pi_{ip}\pi_{pN} - \pi_{pp}\pi_{iN}).$$

Given our construction of the market demand function,[17] it can easily be shown that $\pi_{pN} = 0$. Then, since $\pi_{pp} < 0$, it follows that the derivative under consideration is positive or negative as π_{iN} is positive or negative, respectively. This cross partial is equal to

$$\pi_{iN} = (1-v)(p_i - h_i)q_i^i ,$$

and, since all three factors on the right hand side are positive, it follows that π_{iN} is also positive.

We conclude therefore that market population exerts a positive influence on the optimal input of athletic talent, and hence, on the absolute and relative quality of the club. This hypothesis will be tested empirically in the next chapter.

Other Demand Shifts

Suppose that m is some market variable, other than population, which affects the demand for tickets. Again, we are interested in the qualitative effect of such shifts on the optimal level of team quality. Equivalently, we wish to find the sign of the derivative dx_i^0/dm, and since as before,

$$\text{sgn}(\frac{dx_i^0}{dm}) = \text{sgn}(\pi_{ip}\pi_{pm} - \pi_{pp}\pi_{im}),$$

we must examine the signs of π_{pm} and π_{im}.

We begin with an analysis of π_{pm}, and our approach is via the effect of changes in m on the price elasticity of demand for tickets. In particular if we

---

[17]Our particular specification of the demand function is not necessary for the results that follow. They are more general than this. It is only necessary that $\pi_{pN} \geqslant 0$ or, equivalently, $Q_N \geqslant 0$ and either $Q_{pN} \geqslant 0$ or $\partial e_p/\partial N \leqslant 0$. The demand specification in this model is satisfactory in that $Q_N > 0$ and $Q_{pN} = 0$.

express condition (4-8a) in the form in which it appears in footnote 14 and then apply the chain rule for differentiation, we obtain

$$\pi_{pm} = (1 - v)Q \left[-\frac{p - h}{p} \right] \frac{de_p}{dm} , \qquad (4\text{-}15)$$

which, by inspection, must take the sign opposite to that of de_p/dm. Thus, if the effect of variations in m is to decrease the elasticity of demand, then π_{pm} is positive, and conversely, if the change in m increases demand elasticity, π_{pm} is negative.

Next we examine the other cross partial, π_{im}, which we obtain by differentiating (4-8b) with respect to m:

$$\pi_{im} = (1 - v)(p - h)Q_{im} - G_{im} . \qquad (4\text{-}16)$$

Let us initially assume that the last term on the right side of (4-16) is zero, that is that m has no effect on marginal talent costs. The sign of π_{im} will therefore be positive or negative as variations in m have positive or negative effects, respectively, on the marginal returns to athletic talent, Q_i.

Suppose now that $m \equiv s$, where s is an index of the availability of substitute forms of recreational and entertainment activities in the market. We would expect that an increase in available substitutes would both increase demand elasticity and not increase the marginal returns to improved team quality, that is $de_p/ds > 0$ and $Q_{is} \leqslant 0$, so that $\pi_{ps} < 0$ and $\pi_{is} \leqslant 0$. Thus, by the application of Equation (4-14a), we conclude that $dx^0/ds < 0$: The optimal quality of the team will vary inversely with the range of substitutes available in the market.

On the other hand, any variations in market parameters which decrease the elasticity of demand for tickets, and/or increase the marginal effect of athletic talent, will exert a positive influence on the club's optimal level of quality.

These hypotheses will also be subjected to empirical test in Chapter 5.

Variations in Cost

It can be seen immediately from (4-16) that if $G_{im} > 0$, that is, if variations in m increase the marginal cost of athletic talent, then π_{im} is negative, and $(dx^0/dm) < 0$. Also, if $G_{im} < 0$ then $(dx^0/dm) > 0$. This result is certainly not startling. Intuitively, one would expect increases in the marginal cost of athletic talent to reduce the optimal level of employment of that input, but the empirical question of what particular market variations affect a club's costs of acquiring athletic talent is of some interest.

It is often asserted that professional athletes form preferences among the various professional sports markets on the basis of the potential opportunities for supplementary income. In particular, it is claimed that New York and Los Angeles are the prime employment areas from the standpoint of the professional athlete: New York, because of its advertising and other commercial advantages, and Los Angeles because of its proximity to the television and motion picture industries, in which increasing numbers of professional athletes are employed in the off season. Such preferences, if they exist, might be expected to exert some influence on the club's marginal cost of acquiring and maintaining a given stock of athletic talent.

**Variations in the Visitor's
Gate Share**

Unlike our previous cases, we are not able to make a general prediction about the sign of dx^0/dv, the adjustment derivative for a change in the visitor's share of the net gate revenues. It can easily be shown that $\pi_{pv} = 0$, and that, by (4-14a) the sign of dx^0/dv will be the sign of π_{iv}, which in turn may be written as

$$\pi_{iv} = -(p_i - h_i)Q_i^i + \sum_{j \neq i} N_j (p_j - h_j)q_i^{ji}. \qquad (4\text{-}17)$$

The first term on the right of (4-17) is negative, and the sign of the second term depends upon the signs of the cross effects, the q_i^{ji}. Thus we are not able, in the general case, to uniquely determine the sign of π_{iv}. A special case however may be of interest.

Assume that the i-th club is of very superior athletic quality, in which case we would expect that the marginal cross effects of further increases in its quality, the q_i^{ji}, are predominantly negative. In other words, widening the gap between a superior team and the rest of the league is likely to have a depressing effect on home attendance in the rest of the league. If this is true, we can conclude that, where i is our hypothetical "superior" team, $dx^0/dv < 0$. In other words, the visitor's gate share may be a device for rendering nonoptimal any situation where one club would essentially monopolize most of the scarce athletic talent to an extent that would adversely affect the ticket sales of other league members.

**A Summary of the Model and
Its Implications**

In this chapter we have constructed a static model of optimal team quality in which each club is assumed to act as a Cournot-independent profit maximizer. With the number of teams, their respective monopoly markets, and the schedule of athletic contests taken as given, the model is essentially short run in nature.

Assuming that profit functions are concave in the relevant variables, solution of the model's first order conditions for profit maximization indicates that the optimal level of team quality for an individual club is related to the marginal cost of athletic talent, the sensitivity of demand to variations in team quality, and the price elasticity of demand for tickets.

An analysis of certain comparative statics derivatives indicates that, in particular, the optimal level of team quality is positively related to the population of the market in which the club plays its home games, and negatively related to those characteristics of the market which would tend to increase the price elasticity of demand for the club's product. Thus we conclude that those clubs located in more populous markets and/or in markets where there are few recreational substitutes and where the club's monopoly position is therefore stronger, will tend to be athletically superior to those clubs located in the less attractive markets.

We also conclude that the visitor's share of gate revenues may have the effect of mitigating these interclub differences in optimal team quality.

In Chapter 5, these hypotheses and others will be subjected to empirical test.

5

Some Empirical Evidence in Support of the Model

Our purpose in this chapter is twofold: (1) to construct and estimate an empirical model of demand for attendance at major league baseball games by which to investigate some of the relations that, up to now, have played the role of maintained hypotheses in the development of our argument, and (2) to test both formally and informally some of the implications of the model as derived in the preceding two chapters.

Our data set for this task is composed exclusively of data generated by major league baseball clubs, but in most cases our results can be generalized to apply to other sports as well. Baseball was chosen both because of the availability of the data and because of its relative stability in the postwar period. To a large extent the structures of organized professional football, basketball, and hockey, as well as the rules of play in these sports, have undergone considerable change since World War II. Professional baseball, therefore, provides us with a more stable framework within which to carry out our investigation, a framework which more closely resembles that assumed in the previous chapter's model.

The Demand for In-person Attendance at Major League Baseball Games, 1951-1969

The Structure of the Demand Model

In order to investigate, first, the incentives of the individual club with regard to team quality vis-à-vis competitive equality within the league, and secondly, the extent to which intermarket differences affect the revenue potential of the various clubs, we formulate an empirical model of the demand for seats at major league professional baseball games.

Let us begin by postulating the underlying structure presumed to generate the observed behavior of the purchasers of admission to these games, a structure which, it turns out, enables us to use simple least squares methods to estimate the demand for tickets. This latter point is not insignificant, since most other estimation procedures would require the use of information beyond that which is available, specifically information concerning input costs and broadcast revenues.

We define the following variables appearing in the structural demand model:

A = Total home attendance for a club over the course of the season.

P = The price of admission to the club's home games during the season.

V = The number of club's games televised during the season.

T = The stock of athletic talent employed by the club during the season.

X = The relative quality of the club over the season.

M = A vector of characteristics of the club's market.

Z = A vector of parameters affecting the club's pricing, employment, and broadcasting decisions, but not directly entering the structural demand function. This would include such things as the marginal cost of supplying seats or purchasing athletic talent, and the marginal revenue from the sale of television broadcast rights.

U_k = The random disturbance term affecting the k-th endogenous relation of the model.

The first five of these variables are assumed to be endogenously determined within the model, while M, the vector of market characteristics, is assumed to be exogenous. In a more sophisticated model, one would explicitly recognize the choice of a market as a long run decision variable of the firm, and appropriately include at least certain components of M among the endogenous variables. Here, however, the determination of such things as population, disposable income, and the availability of substitutes in the club's market is assumed to be beyond the scope of the model. Z is also taken as exogenously determined.

The structure of the model can be expressed in the following general system of equations, where the negative subscripts indicate lagged values of the variable:

$$A = A(P, V, X, M, U_a). \tag{5-1}$$

$$P = P(V, T, A_{-1}, M, Z, U_p). \tag{5-2}$$

$$V = V(P, T, A_{-1}, M, Z, U_v). \tag{5-3}$$

$$T = T(P, V, A_{-1}, M, Z, U_t). \tag{5-4}$$

$$X = X(T, U_x). \tag{5-5}$$

Our primary interest lies in the estimation of relation (5-1), the demand equation, and this task is considerably facilitated by the structure outlined above. The reader will note that Equations (5-2) through (5-5) represent an independent subbloc of the model, and that their solution is logically prior to the solution of the demand equation, and thus of the model as a whole. The logical priority, of course, reflects the causal structure of the mechanism which generates the demand for tickets: The pricing and broadcasting decisions and the decision to purchase a given stock of athletic talent are made by the club prior (in both a logical and temporal sense) to the sale of adminissions to any games. These decisions are made before the season starts, and they are assumed to remain unaltered over the course of that season.[1] This is reflected in the model by the independent, mutually determinate subsystem formed by relations (5-2), (5-3), and (5-4). The presence of the lagged value of attendance in these relations may be taken to indicate that the decision rules for pricing, broadcasting, and stocking athletic talent may include an attempt to forecast future attendance demand from past experience.[2] It is also clear that the solution of Equation (5-5) for Q follows immediately, given the solution of the three simultaneous equations in P, V, and T.

We conclude therefore that the model forms a recursive, or more specifically a bloc recursive system.[3] The first bloc consists of Equations (5-2) − (5-4), wherein P, V, and T are simultaneously determined. The second bloc, the solution of which depends upon the first, is the single Equation (5-5). Finally the third bloc, the demand Equation (5-1), may be solved once the values conceptually "solved for" in the other two blocs are "plugged in." The solution of the first two blocs of the model is not generally observable, since we lack information concerning many of the components of the vector, Z.[4] We can, however, observe the values of P, V, and X generated by this solution, and this is sufficient to allow us to estimate the demand equation via the application of ordinary least squares techniques.

It is this approach that we have taken in estimating an empirically suitable formulation of Equation (5-1). In particular, two forms of the demand function are specified: The first is a simple linear form with seasonal home attendance as the dependent variable; the second is also linear, but with home attendance per capita as the dependent variable.[5] The latter form, as will be seen below, enables us to obtain a more satisfactory point estimate of the price effect on demand by eliminating the problem of multicollinearity between that variable and population. It also follows more closely the demand formulation employed in the preceding chapter.

---

[1]This condition may not be strictly followed in practice. For example, clubs may occasionally make minor alterations in their broadcast schedules during the playing season. They are also permitted, by league rules, to engage in some limited purchasing of (or trading for) additional athletic talent. Our model ignores this type of behavior.

[2]Perhaps a more complete specification of the model would include an explicit rule for forecasting attendance, say $A_f = A_f(P, T, V, A_{-1}, A_{-2}, \ldots, A_{-t})$, and thus replace A_{-1} in the above system by A_f. This would not substantively alter the model.

[3]See, for example, Wonnacot and Wonnacot [1970], p. 195.

[4]Such a solution would require the construction of an index to measure T, the stock of athletic talent under contract to the club. This in itself would be no mean task, since T is a multidimensional variable, certain components of which would necessarily require subjective evaluation.

[5]Logarithmic transformations were also employed, but the resulting estimates were entirely unsatisfactory and are not reported here.

The Data

A combination of cross section and time series data was used in the estimation. The sample included 282 observations on sixteen major league clubs, eight from the NL and eight from the AL, over the period 1951-1969. Since many of the series used in estimation were constructed from raw data, a brief explanation of these variables is warranted.

Information gleaned from many sources, among them, *The Sporting News, The Official Baseball Guide*, and the press guides of the various clubs, was used in constructing the price series for each club. The major problem in constructing such a series is that the clubs engage in multipart pricing, each price nominally corresponding to the quality of seat purchased.[6] Ideally one would like to obtain a measure of the average ticket price, but without revenue data, such an average revenue figure is not directly obtainable. What we have done, therefore, is to calculate a weighted average of prices for each club in each year, the weights being the proportion of seats available in each category. Such a course implicitly assumes that seats are sold in the same proportion in which they are physically available within the stadium. While this is not strictly true, there is no reason to believe that such an assumption introduces any systematic bias into the price series, so that our weighted average price series may serve as a reasonably close proxy for the true average price series.

The income variable used in the demand equation is the "effective buying income per household" for the respective metropolitan areas in the sample, as reported in *Sales Management's* annual "Survey of Buying Power."

The income and price variables were corrected for both intermarket and intertemporal price differences as follows. A time series on the consumer price index by metropolitan area was obtained from the *Handbook of Labor Statistics* [1970] and combined with a cross section index of comparative living costs in various urban areas for the year 1966. This latter figure was reported in the *Statistical Abstract of the United States (1969).* By combining the information in these two indices we were able to construct a composite price index reflecting both temporal and geographical price differences, and whose base was the U.S. urban average consumer price index for the year 1966.

The population variable used in the estimations was the relevant SMSA (Standard Metropolitan Statistical Area) population as reported in *Sales Management* and elsewhere. In some cases, two or more SMSAs were combined when it was felt that the resulting measure would correspond more closely to the actual market from which the club's audience was primarily drawn. For our purposes, therefore, the following SMSAs were combined: San Francisco-Oakland and San Jose; New York and Newark; Baltimore and Washington, D.C.; Los Angeles-Long Beach, and Anaheim-Santa Ana-Garden Grove.

---

[6]We say "nominally" because seat classifications and prices are somewhat arbitrary. Clubs often alter their effective admission price by reclassifying, and repricing, relatively large blocks of seats. In fact, they prefer this method to that of announcing price changes.

One of the more important variables in the demand function, from the standpoint of this research, is a measure of the team's quality relative to the other teams in its league. We have based our index of relative team quality on the figure referred to as "games behind the leader" (GBL), as observed at five monthly intervals over the course of the season.

Initially, one might be inclined to calculate the simple average of these five observations and use it as a (negative) measure of team quality. As will become evident, however, such a procedure is equivalent to an implicit assumption that potential consumers form judgments about a team's quality solely on the basis of its current performance, and that such judgments are changed instantaneously and completely when current performance is altered. Such an assumption of perfectly elastic expectations would seem unwarranted a priori, and can in fact be shown to be a special case of the more general approach presented below, an approach in which past performance as well as current performance, influences consumer evaluations of relative quality.

Let us assume that attendance depends on some expected, or "permanent," team quality as evaluated by potential ticket buyers.[7] Write X_t^* for this expected quality at time t, and X_t for actual quality, both measured in GBL. We postulate the following adjustment processes for the revision of the consumer's expectations of team quality:

$$\Delta X_t^* = \delta(X_t - X_{t-1}^*),\tag{5-6}$$

where $0 \leqslant \delta \leqslant 1$, and $\Delta X_t^* = X_t^* - X_{t-1}^*$. By successive substitution we obtain the following expression of permanent quality at time t as a weighted average of actual past performance:

$$X_t^* = \delta X_t + \delta(1-\delta)X_{t-1} + \delta(1-\delta)^2 X_{t-2} + \dots.\tag{5-7}$$

If attendance in period t is linearly related to this measure of permanent quality by the relation $A_t = h_t + k \cdot X_t^*$, then it can easily be shown that

$$A_t = h_t + k\delta \cdot X_t + (1-\delta) \cdot A_{t-1},\tag{5-8}$$

where h_t is the linear combination of all other factors affecting A_t. In Equation (5-8) both k and the adjustment elasticity, δ, are identified and presumably could be estimated given observations on the A_t's and the corresponding X_t's. Unfortunately, such an approach is not open to us, since as indicated above, our data includes five monthly observations per season on X_t, but only a single observation per season on home attendance. Therefore, in order to make use of all of the available data, and at the same time to avoid suppressing the problem of expectations adjustments, the following procedure was adopted.

---

[7]The analogy with Friedman's permanent income hypothesis will become obvious as we proceed.

Let us subscript and superscript the variables to distinguish between the year (or season) and the month of that season. X_t^m therefore will represent an observation on X at the end of the m-th month of the t-th season, where $m = 1, \dots, 5$. Each X^m is observable, but with respect to attendance, only $A_t = \sum_m A_t^m$, or seasonal attendance can be observed. We can write

$$A_t^1 = h_t^1 + k[\delta X_t^1 + \delta(1-\delta)X_{t-1}^5 + \delta(1-\delta)^2 X_{t-1}^4 + \dots]$$

$$A_t^2 = h_t^2 + k[\delta X_t^2 + \delta(1-\delta)X_t^1 + \delta(1-\delta)^2 X_{t-1}^5 + \dots]$$

$$\begin{matrix} \cdot & \cdot & & \cdot & & \cdot \\ \cdot & \cdot & & \cdot & & \cdot \\ \cdot & \cdot & & \cdot & & \cdot \end{matrix} \qquad (5\text{-}9)$$

$$A_t^5 = h_t^5 + k[\delta X_t^5 + \delta(1-\delta)X_t^4 + \delta(1-\delta)^2 X_t^3 + \dots].$$

Taking the vertical sum of the equations in (5-9) we obtain, on the left side, seasonal attendance, A_t, and on the right side a weighted average of five-period moving averages given by

$$\overline{X}_t = \delta \cdot \overline{X}_t^5 + \delta(1-\delta) \cdot \overline{X}_t^4 + \dots +$$
$$\delta(1-\delta)^4 \cdot \overline{X}_t^1 + \delta(1-\delta)^5 \cdot \overline{X}_{t-1}^5 + \dots, \qquad (5\text{-}10)$$

where $\overline{X}_t^m$ is the five period moving average with its last component the *GBL* observation for the m-th month of the t-th season. Then from (5-9) and (5-10) we can write, for attendance in year t,

$$A_t = H_t + k \cdot \overline{X}_t, \qquad (5\text{-}11)$$

where $H_t = \sum_m h_t^m$. Note that only if $\delta = 1$, that is if revisions of permanent quality are perfectly elastic with respect to current performance, is $\overline{X}_t$ equal to the simple average of *GBL* observed at the five points during the season. In general, however, δ may assume any values between zero and unity. The closer it is to unity, the more elastic are revisions in market evaluations of relative quality, and the greater the weight placed on current performance vis-à-vis past performance. Conversely, the smaller the value of δ, the more inelastic are adjustments, and the greater the relative weight placed on past performance in judging the team's quality.

Unfortunately, δ is not uniquely identified in our model,[8] and hence cannot

---

[8] It is actually overidentified, and thus its value cannot be estimated without further a priori restrictions on the model.

be estimated. In lieu of this, the series given by (5-10) was constructed using six different assumed values of δ, ranging from δ =1.0, to δ = 0.5, and a number of different specifications of the demand function estimated using each of these δ-values. In all cases the "best fit," in the sense of both minimum residual variance for the estimate, and highest *t*-statistic for the test of the null hypothesis, was obtained using a δ equal to 0.7. We therefore have assumed this value of δ in constructing the series given by (5-10) for use in our demand estimates. *GBL*, and thus the series, was taken as a negative number.

Another aspect of the club's quality, applying specifically to a first place team, is the margin by which that team leads the rest of the league. We have measured this margin as the average number of games separating a first place team from the second place team, the averages calculated from monthly observations over the course of the season. The variable is, by definition, zero for any club which has not been a league leader at least at one observation point during the season.

We are also interested in the effect on ticket demand of the pennant race, as distinct from the relative quality of an individual club. We must therefore define a proxy, a *race index*, designed to measure the extent to which a "pennant race" may be said to exist. A number of possibilities were considered for this index. Among those rejected were measures of the variance in winning percentages among the clubs, and measures of average GBL for some specified number of clubs. If either of these measures is calculated on the basis of all clubs in the league, the resulting index may exhibit a bias due to variations in the performance of teams clearly not in the pennant race. A numerical example may clarify this.

Assume that there are five clubs in the league, and that they have each played 40 games. Cases I and II below are two hypothetical league standings after 40 games.[9]

	Case I				Case II		
Team	W–L	GBL	Pct.	Team	W–L	GBL	Pct.
A	24-16	0	0.600	A	25-15	0	0.625
B	23-17	1	0.575	B	24-16	1	0.600
C	23-17	1	0.575	C	18-22	6	0.450
D	22-18	2	0.550	D	18-22	6	0.450
E	8-32	15	0.225	E	18-22	6	0.450

Intuitively, Case I would appear to describe a closer pennant race than would Case II. If, however, we calculate the variance in winning percentage among the five clubs, the result is a lower variance for Case II than for Case I, thus leading to the conclusion that II is the closer race. Similarly, employing an average of *GBL* as our race index leads to the conclusion that the two races are equivalent.

[9] League standings are of course constrained by the requirement that the total number of wins must be equal to the total number of losses.

It is clear that the reason Case I is judged the inferior pennant race is due to the relatively poor performance of Team E in that race. An alternative which immediately suggests itself is the elimination of some arbitrary number of lower division clubs from the calculation of variance or average *GBL*, so that their performance would not affect the race index. Again, however, there is a problem: There is no way to tell, *ex ante*, how many clubs should be excluded from the index.

In view of these difficulties encountered in employing variance or *GBL* in an attempt to construct a race index, we have taken a different tack. An essential aspect of the pennant race is that a close race increases uncertainty of outcome by increasing the *number* of potential winners. We have therefore concentrated on a measure of the number of teams in the pennant race. Though the index derived depends upon some arbitrary operational definition of "in the pennant race," and hence is not a unique measure, it appears to be superior to either of the approaches discussed above.

We observed the league standings at the end of each month of the season, from May through September inclusive. The i-th club was defined as a pennant contender in month m if $GBL_i \leqslant k_m$ where $k_m = 7.5$ for $m =$ June, July, August, and $k_m = 5.0$ for $m =$ May, September. Then the average, over the entire season, of the number of pennant contenders was taken as the pennant race index, and this index was used in the demand estimates presented in Tables 5-1 and 5-2.

Since the effect of the pennant race variable on demand is relatively important for our conclusions, we also estimated the demand relations using three other specifications of the race index. These results are discussed below.

The first of the alternative specifications is a dummy variable which assumes the value of 1 if a pennant race exists at all during the season, and is otherwise 0. The second is the number of months in a given season during which a pennant race exists. So defined, the race index can assume integer values from zero to 5. Finally, the third specification of the index is the number of different teams which occupy the league leadership position over the course of the season.

Also included in the demand equation are indices designed to measure the availability of both direct substitutes, in the form of other professional baseball clubs located in the same market, and indirect substitutes, in the form of other (nonbaseball) professional sports clubs operating in that market. Such an index of substitutes must consider both the existence and the quality of these substitutes, but it was felt that simply weighting each available substitute by a measure of its quality, by its winning percentage for example, would understate the substitution effect of a very poor quality team and perhaps overstate the effect of a superior quality team. In other words, it was felt that although another club winning 75 percent of its games is likely to be a more attractive substitute than one winning 25 percent of its games, the three to one ratio would overstate the difference. The very existence of the substitute should be given some weight over and above its quality.

The index we used, therefore, was not the simple sum of substitute teams weighted by their respective winning percentages, but rather the number of substitute teams in the market *plus* the sum of their respective winning percentages.[10] Thus, for example, for a baseball club playing in a market in which there exist both a professional football team with a winning percentage of 0.50 and a professional basketball team with a winning percentage of 0.60, the index of indirect substitutes would be 1.50 + 1.60 = 3.10. The index for direct substitutes is computed in the same way.

Among the remaining independent variables entering into the demand equation are the following: the number of home games and away games televised by the club, a time trend, the number of years the club has been located in its market, and a set of dummy variables corresponding to the existence of a new stadium, a league champion, a world champion, and a change in the number of scheduled games from 154 to 162. This latter schedule change was made in 1961 by the American League and in 1962 by the National League, and in both cases was accompanied by the addition of two expansion clubs. The effects of expanding the schedule and the league are, therefore, both reflected in this dummy and without further data neither is separately identifiable.

Demand Estimates

As indicated above, the demand model was estimated in two forms, one with total seasonal home attendance as the dependent variable (Form A), the other with seasonal home attendance per capita (attendance divided by market population) as the dependent variable (Form B). Each form was estimated for the entire sample of 282 observations on 16 clubs, as well as separately for the eight American League clubs (145 observations), and the eight National League clubs (137 observations). The estimates of Form A and Form B of the demand equation, along with the *t*-values for the null hypothesis and the coefficients of multiple correlation, appear in Tables 5-1 and 5-2, respectively.

Some of the more pronounced differences in coefficients and *t*-values among the various samples can be explained on the basis of individual sample peculiarities. For example, the "Average Lead" and "World Champion" variables have much smaller coefficients and *t*-values in the American League estimates than in the estimates based upon the other two samples. This is true especially in Table 5-1. Such a discrepancy is probably the result of the dominance of the AL by a single team, the New York Yankees, over most of the sample period. As a

---

[10] Such a procedure is equivalent to the following assumption. If two separate variables, one measuring the number of substitutes and one measuring their quality (winning percentage), were included in the demand function, then their estimated coefficients should be equal. This procedure was, in fact, initially employed with the result that the hypothesis of equal coefficients could be rejected in only one case out of four. Thus we feel safe in constructing the index as described in the text. The reason for not using the two variable approach in the final estimate was their obviously high degree of multicollinearity.

Table 5-1

The Demand for Seats at Major League Baseball Games

Form A: Dependent Variable = Seasonal Home Attendance (10^3)

Independent Variable	Both Leagues	American League	National League
Relative Team Quality	25.341*	24.04*	22.86*
	(10.52)	(8.57)	(5.30)
Average Lead	23.711*	8.14	43.88*
	(2.25)	(0.67)	(2.47)
League Champion (dummy)	72.299	189.63**	−50.75
	(0.99)	(2.04)	(0.46)
World Champion (dummy)	209.184**	51.42	347.88*
	(2.27)	(0.43)	(2.49)
Race Index	14.733	13.68	27.93
	(0.99)	(0.77)	(1.13)
Population (10^6)	40.597*	22.84**	40.95**
	(4.98)	(2.27)	(1.99)
Direct (baseball) Substitutes Index	−150.1*	−142.8*	−67.2
	(5.64)	(4.92)	(0.77)
Indirect (nonbaseball) Substitutes Index	26.68**	14.6	28.3
	(1.76)	(0.80)	(1.12)
Household Real Disposable Income (10^3)	13.923	4.02	32.07
	(0.74)	(0.17)	(1.02)
Average Ticket Price	0.956	−0.714	2.58**
	(1.14)	(0.72)	(1.80)
Home Games Televised (No.)	−3.708*	−0.46	−6.53*
	(3.57)	(0.31)	(3.82)
Away Games Televised (No.)	−4.733*	−2.16	−4.86*
	(4.45)	(1.50)	(2.77)
Year in City ($\leqslant 5$)	−102.667*	−125.72*	−87.03*
	(5.04)	(4.79)	(2.50)
New Stadium (dummy)	633.007*	N.A.	516.89*
	(3.92)		(2.89)
Schedule Change and Expansion (dummy)	−82.591**	−56.93	−128.84
	(1.65)	(0.96)	(1.60)
Constant	1566.52*	2005.01*	945.51**
	(4.78)	(5.12)	(1.66)
R^2	0.6270	0.6185	0.6953

*Coefficient significantly different from zero at 99 percent level of confidence.

**Coefficient signficantly different from zero at 95 percent level of confidence.

consequence of this dominance, there is much less variance in these variables within the American League sample, and this in turn is reflected in the smaller estimated t-values since the latter are inversely related to sample variance.

Similarly, the negative value of the estimated coefficient of the "League Champion" dummy for the National League estimates in Table 5-1 may reflect

Table 5-2
The Demand for Seats at Major League Baseball Games
Form B: Dependent Variable = Attendance per Capita

Independent Variable	Both Leagues	American League	National League
Relative Team Quality	0.01073* (5.02)	0.00775* (4.22)	0.01697* (3.95)
Average Lead	0.02014** (2.15)	0.00879 (1.11)	0.02911** (1.65)
League Champion (dummy)	0.04719 (0.74)	0.01306 (0.22)	0.02576 (0.24)
World Champion (dummy)	−0.00131 (0.02)	−0.00354 (0.05)	0.01155 (0.08)
Race Index	−0.00470 (0.36)	0.01340 (1.13)	−0.01885 (0.75)
Direct (baseball) Substitutes Index	−0.07059* (3.10)	−0.04433** (2.33)	−0.13391* (2.52)
Indirect (nonbaseball) Substitutes Index	−0.08545* (6.74)	−0.08310* (7.58)	−0.08401* (3.36)
Household Real Disposable Income (10^3)	0.00714 (0.38)	−0.01209 (0.70)	0.06518** (1.85)
Average Ticket Price	−0.00196* (2.69)	−0.00032 (0.51)	−0.00493* (3.41)
Home Games Televised (No.)	−0.00309* (4.02)	−0.00229* (3.30)	−0.00406* (2.39)
Away Games Televised (No.)	−0.00292* (3.04)	0.0045 (0.47)	−0.00736* (4.32)
Time Trend (t-1950)	−0.00229 (0.34)	−0.00427 (0.70)	0.00552 (0.44)
Years in City ($\leqslant 5$)	−0.13037* (7.22)	−0.11699* (6.86)	−0.08672* (2.58)
New Stadium (dummy)	−0.01513 (0.11)	N.A.	0.03184 (0.18)
Schedule Change and Expansion (dummy)	−0.02704 (0.47)	−0.06431 (1.24)	−0.03413 (0.33)
Constant	2.0040* (6.14)	1.6120* (5.33)	2.1281* (3.63)
R^2	0.5768	0.6995	0.6115

*Coefficient significantly different from zero at 99 percent level of confidence.
**Coefficient significantly different from zero at 95 percent level of confidence.

the fact that the reigning champion in the NL seldom repeated its achievement in the current season. Thus, the unitary value of this dummy was usually associated with a decrease in team quality and therefore with a decline in attendance. Other instances of pronounced intersample differences in the estimates are most likely due to similar sample peculiarities.

We now turn to an interpretation of these results.

Returns to Winning Versus
Competitive Equality

Among the more important implications of the model, for our purposes, are those concerning the incentives of the individual club. Specifically, we are concerned with the returns to supplying a winning team vis-à-vis the returns to supplying a close pennant race. From Tables 5-1 and 5-2 we see that the "relative team quality" variable enters each demand specification with the a priori expected sign, and with an estimated coefficient which is statistically significant at the 99 percent level of confidence. Note also the relative uniformity of the coefficient, especially for Form A, among the various data sets.[11]

It may be instructive to translate these results into revenue figures in order to grasp their importance with respect to the distribution of league profits. To simplify, let us compare two clubs, one a contender and one an also ran. Club X, the contender, is on the average 5 games behind the leader whereas Club Y is on the average 15 games behind. The absolute attendance form of the demand equation estimate suggests that, other things equal, the seasonal attendance of Club X will exceed that of Club Y by about 253,000. At an average ticket price of about $2.50 and with 80 percent of the gate retained by the home team this implies a revenue difference of in excess of $500,000, or nearly 10 percent of the total revenue for a representative baseball club.[12] Using the estimates for the per capita form of the demand equation, the attendance, and hence revenue, differences are even greater. If X and Y are each located in a metropolitan area of 2.5 million people, the approximate 1970 median market population of our sample, the expected attendance difference would be about 275,000 implying a revenue difference of about $550,000.[13]

Our other index of team quality, the *average lead* of a first place team over the second place team during the season, is designed to tell us something about the effects of winning by a close margin versus winning by a large margin. As indicated above, Rottenberg bases much of his argument on the maintained

---

[11]This observed uniformity holds not only for the sample reported here, but for estimates based on a number of other samples also. In many cases with both different sample sizes and different specifications of the demand equation, the estimated coefficient of the relative quality variable was invariably quite close to 25, and always statistically significant.

[12]See Table 2-3, Chapter 2 for estimates of the revenues of a "typical" club. Long run revenue differences among clubs would of course tend to zero if the average talent distribution approached equality. This, however, is not historically the case. In the 25 year postwar period, New York and Chicago, among the American League clubs have finished on the average 5 and 7 games behind respectively, while for St. Louis/Baltimore, Washington/Minnesota, and Philadelphia/Kansas City/Oakland the average GBLs are 14.8, 14.8, and 19.8 respectively. This implies a fairly skewed distribution of league revenues.

[13]Using Form B, the more populous the cities, the larger the attendance, and revenue, difference. For example, for two cities of 3 million population these differences would be 330,000 and $660,000 respectively.

hypothesis that the returns to a narrow victory are larger. Such a hypothesis does not appear to merit support in light of our estimates. In both forms of the demand function this variable has a statistically significant effect for both the combined and the National League samples. However, its sign is opposite that which Rottenberg would presumably expect and, contrary to his belief, demand for tickets to the games of a first place club seems to increase as its lead over the second place club is extended.

In order to ascertain whether the nominal title of "League Champion" or "World Champion" affects demand for tickets, these two effects were included as dummy variables, taking on the value of 1 if the club is the reigning champion, and 0 otherwise. Though these variables do not appear to exert any significant effect on demand estimated on a per capita basis, Table 5-2, they do show up as significant in some cases when absolute attendance is used. The implication is that the nominal title of "Champion" may serve as a form of advertising for the club, and if this is true, it provides an additional incentive for winning.

The existence of a close pennant race, on the other hand, does not appear to have any significant effect on the individual club's demand. The coefficient of our pennant race index is not significantly different from zero in any of the six estimations, and in two of them it has the "wrong" sign. Furthermore, this conclusion holds not only for the particular specification of the race index in Tables 5-1 and 5-2, but also for estimates based upon the three alternate race index specifications above.[14] In no case does this variable exert a statistically significant effect on attendance demand, and in many cases its sign is the opposite of what is usually predicted.

We must conclude on the basis of this evidence, therefore, that the incentive of the individual club is to win, and not necessarily to win by a close margin. The existence of a close pennant race benefits only those clubs in the race, that is, clubs that are (potential) winners, and does not affect other clubs. The fact that there are other, more direct, returns to winners in the form of playoff money and other incentives only serves to strengthen the above conclusion.

The Effects of Exogenous, Intermarket Differences

Our estimates also have implications for the effects of certain exogenous differences among the markets in which the clubs operate. Among these factors are population, the availability of substitutes, both direct and indirect, and disposable income.

---

[14] A measure of the variance in winning percentage among all league members was also used as a race index proxy in an earlier (and quite different) specification of the demand function. In that case also the effects were statistically insignificant.

The absolute attendance form of the demand equation Table 5-1 suggests that each additional one million people in the club's market area increases demand for tickets by about 40,000 per season. The estimated coefficient is significant at the 99 percent level of confidence.[15]

Also, given the indices of direct (baseball) and indirect (other professional sports) market competition discussed above, these variables appear to exert a significant influence on the demand for seats. The effect of direct competition from another major league baseball club is statistically significant and of the expected sign in either form of the demand estimate. The magnitude of the estimate suggests that the existence of another major league club in the same market, and winning half of its games, reduces demand by 230,000 according to Form A, or by 265,000 using Form B for a metropolitan area with a population of 2.5 million.

With regard to the index of indirect competition from other professional sports clubs in a given metropolitan area, Form A of the demand estimate would seem to suggest that the direction of its effect is the opposite of that expected. The estimated coefficient is, however, misleading since there is a strong multicollinearity between the index and the population variable.[16] This multicollinearity problem is not present in Form B, and there the estimated coefficients are statistically significant, and of the a priori expected sign. The figures suggest that the existence of an average major league professional sports attraction, other than baseball, reduces the demand for tickets to baseball games by about 300,000 assuming a metropolitan area population of 2.5 million.

In neither form of the demand equation does household disposable income appear to play any significant role.

Decision Variables: Pricing and Television

Multicollinearity with population also precludes an estimation of the price effect in the absolute attendance form of the demand equation. This problem is of course not present in the per capita estimates, and we obtain statistically significant coefficients with negative signs, as predicted by economic theory. In fact, using the full sample estimate in Table 5-2, and evaluating at the sample mean, we obtain a point estimate of price elasticity equal to 0.93. This is encouraging, for if the marginal cost of supplying additional consumers is low, as

---

[15]If Form B of the demand estimate is used, the implied effect of population differences is much greater. Average per capita attendance over the sample is 0.43. This is of course per capita demand for tickets evaluated at the mean values of the arguments in Form B of the demand equation. The implication is, that in the vicinity of this mean, an additional one million population generates demand for an additional 430,000 seats. Such an extrapolation, however, may not be warranted, and we feel more comfortable with the estimate derived from demand Form A.

[16]See, for example, Table 2-1 in Chapter 2.

we would expect it to be, an optimal pricing policy on the part of the club would imply a price elasticity close to unity.

Televising games has the expected effect on demand: According to Table 5-1, each additional televised game reduces the in-person audience by about four thousand.[17] It is also interesting to note that, contrary to the conventional belief, the televising of road games appears to have roughly the same effects on demand as the televising of home games.

These estimated effects of televising games on the demand for in-person attendance also enable us to indirectly measure the marginal revenues from the club's sale of the television rights to its games. Suppose that the only variable cost incurred by the club in televising its games is the resulting loss of live audience. Then we can calculate the marginal cost of televising an additional game, and, if the club behaves optimally with respect to its broadcast policy, this marginal cost should be approximately equal to the marginal revenues generated by the last game televised by the club.

For example, referring to Table 5-1, we find that televising an additional game results in the loss of about 4000 paid admissions. At an average ticket price of $2.50, the implied marginal revenue of the broadcast is $8000 when the home gate share is 80 percent.

If we make analogous calculations using the results of our per capita demand estimates as shown in Table 5-2, we can calculate the implied effects of population on marginal television revenues, since this latter will be proportional to market population. As Table 5-1 indicates, the real marginal cost of an additional televised game will be the loss of about three thousand paid admissions per one million of market population, and, at the same ticket price assumed above, this implies a marginal television revenue of $6000 per one million population.

Miscellaneous Variables Affecting Demand

Evidence from a variety of recent surveys has often been interpreted as indicative of a long run secular decline in the popularity of baseball, and in order to test this assertion, we have inserted a time trend into our estimate of per capita demand. We conclude that, while the above hypothesis may be true of professional baseball's *relative* popularity, our results yield no evidence of a secular decline in the absolute level of demand for baseball tickets. Any downward trend, if it exists, can be explained in terms of the economic variables in the model, without resort to a temporal shift in tastes.

One other time-related phenomenon, however, does apparently exert a negative influence on demand. This is the number of years (up to five) that the

---

[17]The negative effect is slightly larger using the estimates in Table 5-2 and a metropolitan area population of 2.5 million.

club has been in a given market. As the estimates in both Tables 5-1 and 5-2 indicate, this variable has a statistically significant, and relatively strong, effect on demand. This may partially explain the recent trends toward increased franchise shifting by club owners.

Finally, our dummy variable indicating an increase in the number of scheduled games from 154 to 162 has an estimated negative effect on demand (though this effect is statistically insignificant in all but one case). To explain this we recall that the schedule change was accompanied by league expansion from eight to ten clubs. Thus while each team played four more home games, an additional nine home games were played against the typically noncontending expansion teams, and the net effect appears to have been to diminish total seasonal attendance.

*Comparison with Demand for Tickets
to Professional Basketball Games*

It is of some interest to compare our baseball demand estimates with those of Noll and Okner ([1971], pp. 6ff.) for professional basketball, though there is a technical defect in their procedure in that stadium capacity, a supply parameter, appears as a variable in their "demand" relation. As a result, what they have in reality estimated is a reduced form attendance relation rather than the structural demand equation. They also fail to include a number of variables which appear in our estimates, namely, televised games, a pennant race index, and many of our dummy variables.

Nevertheless, considering that the comparison is between two different professional sports, the estimates are remarkably similar. Noll and Okner's estimates were based on a sample of 22 of the 25 professional basketball teams operating during the 1969-70 season. Their results indicate, as did ours, a significant positive effect on demand of team quality and population, and a significant negative effect for the number of years in the city and the number of professional teams in the area, though they did not distinguish, as we did in this latter variable, between basketball and other professional sports.

Some Evidence on the Influence of Market Variables on Team Quality

A Formal Hypothesis Test

We now propose to test some hypotheses generated by our model, and derived in Chapter 4, namely that certain market differences give rise to differences in the optimal level of team quality. We will confine our attention here to intermarket differences in population and the availability of substitute forms of entertainment, both direct and indirect. The model predicts that population should exert a positive influence on the optimal quality of the club, while the existence and quality of substitutes should have a negative effect.

We take, as our measure of team quality in any given year, the proportion of games won by that team, say W_t^i, for the i-th club in the t-th year, and we define the following variables presumed to influence W_t^i:

N_t^i = Population of the i-th club's market, in millions.

D_t^i = Proxy for the availability and quality of direct (baseball) substitutes in the i-th club's market.

I_t^i = Proxy for the availability and quality of indirect (nonbaseball) substitutes in the i-th club's market.

W_{t-1}^i = The lagged value of W_t^i.

The variables D and I are the same indices as those used in the demand function for direct and indirect substitutes, respectively, but here they are corrected for market population in order to avoid problems of multicollinearity with N. The inclusion of W_{t-1}^i as an explanatory variable reflects the influence of the club's existing stock of playing talent which is largely carried over from one season to the next.

Using a sample of 282 observations on 16 major-league baseball clubs covering the period 1951-1969, the following regression equation is obtained (with t-values in parentheses):

$$W^i = 0.178 + 0.0035\,N^i - 0.034\,D^i + 0.028\,I^i + 0.58\,W_{-1}^i$$

$$(7.63)^* \quad (3.15)^* \quad (1.88)^{**} \quad (3.47)^* \quad (12.41)^*$$

$$(R^2 = 0.4492). \qquad (5\text{-}12)$$

Before interpreting these results the reader should be forewarned about some of the statistical difficulties encountered in attempting to estimate (5-12). First, the coefficient of W_{-1}^i is likely to be biased upward so that the estimate of 0.58 is probably an overestimate of the true value of the coefficient. This is a general problem encountered whenever a lagged value of the dependent variable is included as an explanatory variable and when the two are assumed a priori to be positively related:[18]

Secondly, as indicated by the relatively low value of R^2, there are many factors influencing W which are not included in our specification of (5-12). However, if these excluded influences are purely random, or more generally, if they are orthogonal to (uncorrelated with) the included variables, then their

---

[18] See Johnston ([1960], p. 214-15) for an explanation of this.

exclusion does not exert any bias on the estimated coefficients. A priori this seems likely to be the case. Many purely random events, such as injuries to key players and unexpectedly poor, or good, athletic performances, exert an undeniably large effect on the team's actual performance. Also the quality of other league members, as determined by both systematic and random influences, can affect W^i, but here again there is no reason to expect that this effect should be anything but orthogonal to the independent variables included in (5-12).

If the orthogonality assumption is reasonably accurate, then we should not be overly concerned with the relatively low value of R^2, for we are not attempting to explain completely the variations in W, but rather to test its sensitivity to certain specific factors.

Finally, the third, and possibly the most serious statistical problem which we encounter, is the familiar least squares bias arising from an incomplete specification of the model's structure. In particular, if relations analogous to (5-12) exist for other professional sports clubs in the same market, then it can be shown that the variables D and I will be positively correlated with the disturbance term. This in turn will lead to an overestimate of their coefficients when single equation, ordinary least squares techniques are used in estimation.[19]

Consider intuitively the following extreme case. Population exerts a strong positive influence on the optimal team quality of both the football club and the baseball club which coexist in any given market. Using cross section data for a number of market areas, we would expect to find a net positive correlation between the quality of the baseball team and the quality of the football team located in the same city. Even though, other things equal, the coexistence of a strong football team exerts a negative influence on the baseball team's optimal quality, the influence may appear to be positive when the baseball team's quality is simply regressed on that of the football team.

This may in fact be the explanation of the a priori unexpected positive sign of the coefficient of I, the indirect substitutes index, in Equation (5-12). In order to get an unbiased estimate of the effects of indirect substitutes on team quality a much more complex, multi-equation structural model would have to replace our single equation. This, however, would introduce even further problems, since the same exogenous variables would appear in every equation, thus rendering the system nonidentifiable.

With these cautions in mind let us examine the implications of our estimated Equation (5-12). All coefficients, with the exception of the coefficient of the indirect substitutes term as noted above, have the a priori expected sign and are statistically significant at the 99 percent (*) or 95 percent (**) level of confidence. These results therefore lend some empirical support to the model developed in Chapter 4.

It may be helpful to translate the effect of population on optimal team quality into its implications for intermarket revenue differences. Let us, for

---

[19]See, for example, Christ [1966], pp. 457ff.

simplicity, assume two clubs located in markets which are identical in all respects except for a difference in population of five million people. This population difference will have two effects on demand: a direct effect, and an indirect effect via its implications for optimal team quality. From our estimate of the absolute attendance form of the demand equation, we can conclude that the direct effect of the difference in population is a 200,000 attendance difference. Further, from (5-12) the 5 million population difference results in a difference of 0.018 in winning percentage between the two clubs, which in turn implies a 3 game difference, on the average, in the league standings. Using the point estimate of the coefficient of relative team quality in the demand equation, this implies an additional attendance difference of about 75,000 for a total attendance difference of 275,000. At a $2.50 average ticket price, and a home gate share of 80 percent, this suggests a revenue difference of $550,000 per year. Since team quality is not a free good, the profit difference would not be as large in magnitude, but it should still lead us to conclude that the intraleague distribution of profits may be quite skewed.

The figures above are of course meant to be interpreted as long-run averages.

Some Additional Evidence

In addition to the formal evidence presented above, the history of major league baseball provides some less formal, but rather interesting case studies of managerial behavior which can be interpreted in the light of our model. We will examine three of these cases here: (1) the behavior of Branch Rickey in his role as General Manager of the St. Louis Cardinals and the Brooklyn Dodgers, respectively, (2) certain of the operations of Connie Mack as owner of the Philadelphia Athletics, and (3) the Kansas City Athletics-New York Yankees relationship during the late 1950s.

Branch Rickey

Branch Rickey is widely recognized as perhaps one of the most astute executives in the history of major league baseball. In his role as General Manager he was the prime decision maker in matters concerning the development and employment of playing talent, first for the St. Louis Cardinals and later for the Brooklyn Dodgers. A contrast of his operations with these two different clubs provides some interesting evidence in support of our model.

When Rickey came to St. Louis in 1917, the city, though one of the smallest market areas in major league baseball, was home not only to the Cardinals of the National League, but also to the Browns of the American League. Early in his career, Rickey recognized the near impossibility of competing for playing talent with the clubs in the more lucrative markets. An example of his predicament is given by Allen ([1961], pp. 87-88):

If the Cardinals were to make a modest offer for a minor-league player, the club owning that player's contract would immediately telegraph the news of the bid to the (New York) Giants. Then John McGraw (the Giants' Manager), aware how shrewd a judge of talent Rickey was, would top the offer and the Giants would get the player.

Rickey's reaction to this situation was to organize baseball's first, and for many years, most effective, farm system as a source of playing talent. As a result of this vertical integration, the Cardinals became a perennial league power, and they achieved this while purchasing only one established player during the entire twenty-five years of Rickey's tenure.[20] They, in fact, became exporters of developed major league stars to other clubs, clubs with which an established player's marginal revenue product was apparently higher.

A list of Rickey exports during this period is indeed impressive. It includes the sale of Rogers Hornsby and Johnny Mize to the New York Giants (the latter at a then astronomical price of $52,500), Dizzy Dean and Rip Collins to the Chicago Cubs, Joe Medwick and Mickey Owen to the Brooklyn Dodgers, Preacher Roe to the Pittsburgh Pirates, and Jim Bottomley to the Cincinnati Reds.[21] Rickey's own "offhand estimate" of the net revenues generated by the Cardinal farm system under his direction was somewhere between two-and-one-half and three million dollars.[22] In spite of his financial success and the success of the Cardinals' teams, however, Rickey became the target of increasing criticism from St. Louis fans for his seeming lack of "baseball sentiment" in selling established stars to rival clubs.[23]

In 1942, Rickey resigned his post with the Cardinals and took a similar position with the Brooklyn Dodgers, a club which had narrowly edged the Cardinals in the 1941 pennant race. Ironically, the Dodgers' victory had been due in large part to the players they had purchased from Rickey, among them Joe Medwick, Mickey Owens, Herman Franks, and Pete Reiser.[24]

Once established in the more lucrative New York market, Rickey drastically altered his managerial strategy, and in fact became a net purchaser of playing talent, acquiring such established stars as Ralph Branca, Rocky Bridges, Preacher Roe, Billy Cox, and Andy Pafko. He also purchased the minor league contracts of a number of future Brooklyn Dodger luminaries, including Pee Wee Reese, Billy Loes, Duke Snider, and Gil Hodges.[25] In contrast to the St. Louis

---

[20] Voigt [1970], p. 160.

[21] Lieb [1944b], p. 87.

[22] Mann [1957], p. 228.

[23] Lieb [1944b], p. 87.

[24] Voigt [1970], p. 160.

[25] Meany [1953], pp. 176ff.

operation, these players were nearly all retained by the Dodger club for the duration of their productive careers.

Rickey's behavior fits quite comfortably into our model. In the relatively poor St. Louis market, a star player's potential revenue product would be less than it might be in a richer market; hence Rickey found it profitable to sell many of the players developed in the Cardinal farm system, rather than to retain their services himself. In Brooklyn, however, where the revenue potential of star players was undoubtedly higher than in most other markets, Rickey's approach was to build a winning team, first by purchasing the contracts of many established players, and secondly, by developing and retaining new potential stars within the Brooklyn organization.

Connie Mack

Connie Mack, the owner and manager of the American League's Philadelphia Athletics for nearly half a century, was noted for his ability to build a contending team on a relatively small budget by acquiring the raw playing talent from which he developed a number of star players.[26]

In the early 1920s, Mack began building the nucleus of the only legitimate challenger to the New York Yankee powerhouses of the 1920s and 1930s. In the process he obtained and developed such players as Al Simmons, Mickey Cochrane, Lefty Grove, Jimmy Foxx, Jimmy Dykes, Max Bishop, and George Earnshaw. He also acquired two of the game's established greats, Ty Cobb and Tris Speaker.

As a result the Athletics were strong contenders in the 1925-28 period and won three consecutive American League pennants between 1929 and 1931. But while the Yankee teams of the same era were drawing well over one million paid admissions per year, Mack's clubs were averaging barely over 700,000. Philadelphia attendance in fact declined during the three pennant years from 840,000 to 627,000. At the same time Mack's payroll costs were increasing rapidly. Not a single Athletics' player was paid less than $10,000, and several stars such as Simmons ($33,000), Grove ($20,000), and Cochrane ($20,000) commanded salaries that were quite high by current standards.[27]

Mack began to feel the acute financial pinch at the same time as his clubs were winning pennants. In terms of our model, the quality of his team had surpassed that which was optimal for his market. This was further magnified by the onset of the Great Depression when the Athletics attendance figures dropped below 300,000.[28]

Mack's reaction was predictable: He began selling the contracts of his star

---

[26]Voigt [1970], p. 184.

[27]Lieb [1944a], p. 255.

[28]In contrast, Yankee attendance during the Depression held at about 800,000 per season.

players to clubs in other markets. In 1933, Simmons, Dykes, and Mule Haas were sold to the Chicago White Sox for $150,000, though these players were still in their prime. Cochrane was sold to Detroit for $100,000; Grove, Bishop, and Rube Walberg were sold to Boston for $125,000; Foxx was sold to the same club for $150,000; and Earnshaw went to Chicago for $20,000.[29]

Connie Mack learned by experience the difficulty of maintaining a consistently superior team in a market with limited revenue potential. His actions like those of Branch Rickey are quite consistent with the implications of our model.

The Athletics-Yankees Relationship of the Late 1950s

Connie Mack eventually sold his franchise, and in 1955 the club was moved to Kansas City. The behavior of the Kansas City management during the late 1950s has led some people to conclude that the Athletics were little more than a Yankee farm club during that period, since nearly all the superior players developed in the Kansas City organization were traded or sold to the Yankees while still in their prime. A list of these players would include such Yankee stars as Bobby Shantz, Hector Lopez, Clete Boyer, and Roger Marris.

Writers and baseball fans alike criticized the Athletics' management for what was interpreted as a gross lack of foresight in dealing away potentially great players. However, as our model suggests, this behavior is anything but irrational from the standpoint of the Athletics' ownership, if, as was probably true, these players had potentially greater effects on club revenues in the New York market.

The Kansas City-New York relationship also provides a graphic illustration of the ultimate failure of the reserve system as a tool for impeding the movement of athletic talent to the richer markets. All of the players mentioned above were originally contractually bound to the Athletics by the reserve clause, but economic rationale dictated that these contracts ultimately would be transferred to markets in which their value was higher.

---

[29] Lieb [1944a], pp. 249ff.

6

The Implications of the Model for Efficiency and Equity, and the Role of Public Policy Toward the Professional Team Sports Industry

At this point in the analysis the following conclusions appear warranted both on a priori, theoretical grounds, and on the basis of the empirical results of Chapter 5. First, it has been established that the individual profit maximizing club has little or no incentive to undertake policies designed to promote competitive equality within its league. On the contrary, the empirical estimates of the demand for in-person audience, the implications which these results have for the derived demand for game broadcasts, and the existence of substantial direct payoffs to winning clubs (playoff money) all lead us to conclude that the primary incentive of the club is to field a potentially winning team. But the relative quality of the club, the extent to which it is a winner or a potential winner, is not a direct decision variable for the club; rather it is determined simultaneously by the input decisions of all clubs in the league. In general, the outcome will not be one of competitive equality, in which by definition all clubs are potential winners, but one in which there are both winning teams and losing teams, and hence both more profitable and less profitable franchises. Those factors which produce winning teams, and hence profits, will tend to gravitate toward the markets which yield high returns to a winning club. The losers, in both an athletic and an economic sense, will be the clubs located in markets in which returns to winning are lower.

We have also argued, a priori, that the existence of well developed markets in player contracts and draft rights, precludes the effectiveness of the reserve system in altering the potentially unequal distribution of athletic talent resulting from exogenous differences in market strength among clubs.

These contentions are also borne out by empirical investigation. As both our formal statistical tests and our less formal historical case studies suggest, in spite of one of the most rigid reserve systems in professional sports, variations in market strengths among major league baseball clubs have exerted a significant influence on relative team quality. This influence, when expressed in revenue terms, proves quite substantial.

We have concluded, therefore, that the function of the reserve system is to subsidize all clubs, both the strong and the weak, by enabling them to capture a large share of the rents generated by athletic talent as a specialized factor of production. The existing labor market institutions ensure the viability of the league, but in so doing they create the serious equity problems which have recently culminated in various court tests of the reserve system. In addition, the reserve rules, the territorial rights agreements, and the entry barriers erected by the league to control the total supply of the product, together endow the suppliers with monopoly and monopsony power, the exercise of which leads to allocative inefficiency.

For these reasons it appears that changes in our present public policy, a policy which implicitly condones these activities, are warranted. In particular, we suggest that both the allocative and the distributive characteristics of this market could be improved by policies designed to increase the level of economic competition among professional sports clubs. As we shall attempt to demonstrate, these policies could be constructed in such a way that they would simultaneously increase the level of sporting competition as well.

Given the political constraints imposed upon attempts at realistic policy formulation, the quantum jump to economically competitive input and output markets for professional sports may be an impossibility; it nevertheless provides an ideal against which other, more politically palatable policies may be judged. We therefore turn first to an examination of the market results which we would expect to be generated by an economically competitive professional sports industry, and then to some "second best" policies which accept the inevitability of some degree of monopoly in the industry.

**The Effects of Competitive
Labor Markets Alone**

In the professional team sports industry as presently constituted, monopoly power is exerted in both input and output markets. Let us approach an analysis of the nature and characteristics of full, economically competitive equilibrium in a stepwise fashion. First, we conceptually eliminate the reserve system and any other barriers to the interclub mobility of athletic talent which are the source of monopsony power on the input side of the market. Simultaneously, we assume that the existing monopoly position of the firms with regard to output is retained. This is generally the policy advocated by the player's associations, and as such merits our critical evaluation. We will then examine the effects of the elimination of barriers to economic competition on the output side of the market as well. These include territorial rights and league control over entry.

In order to facilitate the analysis, we assume that the number and geographical distribution of clubs is given, along with the schedule of games to be played among them, and that units of athletic talent are homogeneous and divisible.[1] The analysis is that of comparative statics, our concern being primarily with the equilibrium itself rather than with the dynamic adjustment process. Let us

---

[1] Below, we will investigate the effects of relaxing these assumptions. Their present role, for the most part, is merely to simplify the presentation of our argument.

further assume that all institutional restrictions on the mobility of athletic talent are eliminated, players thus being free to contract with the club of their choice.[2]

Under these conditions, the industry will be in equilibrium when athletic talent is allocated in such a way that the marginal profits to be gained from increased team quality are the same for all clubs. As we have seen in Chapter 3, this equality at the margin does not imply equality of playing strengths when significant differences exist among the respective markets in which the clubs are located. In fact, one would expect that the resulting distribution of athletic talent and team quality would not differ significantly from that existing under present arrangements. This does not, of course, imply that the elimination of barriers to player mobility would have no effects at all. On the contrary, some major effects are to be expected.

Players' wages, which initially were near the reservation price,[3] will be bid up to the marginal revenue product of athletic talent,[4] which, in equilibrium is the same in all markets. Each club is then essentially a price taker, paying units of athletic talent according to their (equal) alternate productivity. The rents which had previously accrued to the clubs are thus transferred to the players, and as a result the profits of all clubs decline. In fact, given the above conclusion concerning the minimal effects on the distribution of relative team quality, it follows that the entire profit distribution should be shifted downward so that those clubs originally earning normal returns are now faced with losses, and may eventually be forced to leave the league. The clubs in the stronger markets, however, will continue to earn greater than normal returns; and we cannot overlook the possibility of side payments, in the form of a more equal sharing of league revenues, designed to preserve the league's viability. Monopoly profits may still exist, given the organization of the output markets, but the distribution of these profits is altered in favor of the players.

Although it is difficult to formulate a substantive and ethically neutral theory of labor's "exploitation," some brief remarks on the subject are warranted at this point. If, with Mrs. Robinson ([1933], p. 281-82), we define exploitation as any state in which labor's wage falls short of the value of its marginal product (equal to output price times labor's marginal physical product), then the elimination of barriers to the mobility of athletic talent is not sufficient to

---

[2] The length of the contractual period is initially ignored but will be considered later. It is clear that if the period is not very short, the contract itself may be a barrier to the perfect mobility of players.

[3] As we have seen, this may not be strictly true if units of athletic talent are indivisible. A talented player may be considered a supplier of a significant share of total athletic talent, and thus as exerting monopoly power himself. In this case we have the classical bilateral monopoly problem in which the player's wage is indeterminate.

[4] The implications regarding the burden of training costs are initially ignored. They have been dealt with in Chapter 3.

eliminate the exploitation of professional athletes. Indeed, since output markets remain monopolized, equilibrium wages will be equal to labor's marginal revenue product, which, under the usual assumptions about demand, is less than the value of labor's marginal product. Though monopsonistic exploitation is eliminated when wages are equal to the marginal revenue product, Mrs. Robinson's "monopolistic exploitation" still exists. This terminology, however, carries with it unwarranted equity and distributional implications, when what is really being described is a situation of resource misallocation due to imperfections in the output market.[5] As we will argue below, players probably benefit from the monopoly structure of the industry, and hence the term "exploitation" may be misleading.

Another potential effect of economically competitive labor markets is an overall improvement in the quality of professionally employed athletes. It is likely that certain players currently employed by professional sports clubs have become professional athletes because their opportunity cost of doing so is small. If their general skills are such that their expected returns in alternate occupations are low, then the existing wage differential may have been sufficient to attract them into professional sports.[6] Conversely, it is conceivable that many potentially superior athletes are not now attracted into the industry because they find their returns in alternate employment to be greater than those which can be expected in professional sports.

Unless, therefore, the supply of athletic talent is perfectly inelastic, an increase in the average wage of professional athletes could be expected to increase the total supply of players, by attracting those superior athletes whose opportunity costs are high. Then, with athletic competition allocating the limited number of positions on the basis of playing ability, the overall quality of professionally employed athletes must increase.

Though a policy based solely on the elimination of barriers to the mobility of athletic talent may be acceptable on equity and quality grounds, it does not cure the basic allocative inefficiencies associated with the exercise of monopoly power. If, by virtue of territorial rights, the clubs are monopoly sellers in their respective markets, and if the total industry supply of the service is collectively controlled through the league cartel, the supply of the services of professional sports clubs will be less than that required for efficient allocation of resources. Furthermore, we can heuristically compare the inefficiencies in relatively strong markets with those in relatively weak markets. In strong markets where clubs, other things equal, tend to be winners or potential winners, expected demand will be large relative to capacity. (Capacity may be measured by the product of

---

[5] This point is made by Bishop [1967], p. 254.

[6] This may be at least a partial explanation for the disproportionate number of black athletes on the rosters of professional sports clubs. As a result of job discrimination and lack of educational opportunity, their opportunity costs are probably, on the average, far below those of white players. This would also apply to native Latin American players. See Pascal and Rapping [1970], p. 21.

the number of games per season and the physical capacity of the stadium.) This capacity will be rationed among potential consumers at prices which exceed the marginal costs of relaxing the capacity constraint by either scheduling more games or expanding the physical plant.

In the weaker markets there will be, on the average, excess capacity in the form of unfilled seats. The marginal costs of serving additional consumers will be at or near zero and the game takes on the analytical aspects of a public good. Ticket prices, however, will not be set at levels equal to marginal cost, but at the level corresponding to unitary demand elasticity,[7] and thus must be above marginal cost. We can therefore expect excess capacity and inefficiency in these markets.

Even if the clubs engaged in revenue sharing to the extent that intermarket differences, and thus differences in optimal team quality within the league, were minimized so that all clubs were potential winners, the allocational inefficiencies in the industry would not be eliminated. Each club would still be a monopolist in its market, and the league cartel would still control total industry supply.

Still further allocational effects are suggested when we consider the entire professional sports industry, including not only the major professional team sports, but minor team and individual sports as well. As we indicated above, when monopoly elements exist in an economic system, the result will be an inefficient allocation of resources within that system. Resources will be under-allocated to monopoly markets, where the value of their marginal product is high, and overallocated to competitive markets, where the value of their marginal product is consequently lower.

This has an interesting implication for resource allocation within the professional sports industry as a whole. Specifically, the league's monopoly restrictions on entry into the major professional team sports may have diverted resources into other professional sports where their value productivity is considerably lower. Thus, for example, relative to existing demand patterns, we may have an oversupply of less popular spectator sports such as professional bowling and professional tennis, along with the restricted supply of professional baseball, football, hockey, and basketball.

Economic Competition in the Output Market

Let us now assume that all institutional impediments to competition are removed from the output side, as well as from the input side, of the market.

---

[7]The rule for optimal (profit maximizing) pricing by the firm is $P(1 - 1/e) = MC$, where P is price, e is the price elasticity of demand, and MC is marginal costs. When $MC = 0$ and $P \neq 0$ this simplifies to $e = 1$. Intuitively, when marginal costs are zero, we are essentially dealing with a problem in revenue maximization, and this occurs at the point of unitary demand elasticity.

Specifically, we assume that the cartel activity of the league in determining the total supply of the product is eliminated, and that new clubs are allowed to enter without the explicit consent of the existing clubs. The league is no longer endowed with the power to sell franchises, but rather entry is relatively free to entrepreneurs willing to incur the set-up costs associated with fielding a team.[8] Let us further assume that territorial rights are eliminated so that the potential entrant is free to locate in any market, regardless of any prior claim by another club.

To simplify the analysis, athletic talent is again assumed to be available in homogeneous, divisible units. The club is viewed as the producer of a differentiated product, which we can characterize as seats at games, and as facing a profit function concave in the relevant decision variables. Initially we ignore the problem of indivisibilities with respect to the team and the market. These assumptions, and the problems arising when they are relaxed, will be examined in greater detail below.

Conceptually, we again approach the problem of industry equilibrium in stepwise fashion. First, competition is introduced solely on the input side of the market with the resulting equilibrium as described in the foregoing section: namely, a distribution of athletic talent and profits which we a priori expect to be skewed in favor of the so called "rich" markets.

Next we eliminate the monopoly institutions which impede competition in output markets. It is evident that potential entrants will now be attracted to those markets in which excess profits exist. The intermarket differences which lead to intraleague inequality in athletic competition will tend to fade, as the clubs which were, prior to entry, earning greater than normal returns find that they are confronted with a growing array of substitutes for their product. As their effective market is thus eroded, the model of team quality developed in Chapter 4 tells us that their optimal stock of athletic talent will tend to fall. As a result, the clubs which operate in markets heretofore characterized as "poor" may find themselves becoming potential winners, for, as a consequence their relative quality must increase. Since revenues display a strong positive relation to relative quality, these clubs will also find their profitability increasing. Entry into the rich markets can therefore be expected to redistribute both relative team quality and profits to the clubs in poorer markets.

If entry into the rich markets proceeds to the point at which clubs in the previously poor markets are earning excess profits, then new clubs would also be attracted into these latter markets. The entry process must continue until rates of return are equal for all clubs, and equal to returns in similar investment opportunities elsewhere in the economy. Since this will also be the point at which differences in market strength have disappeared, it also follows that in full competitive equilibrium, the optimal stock of athletic talent is the same for each club. No long run differences in team strength are to be expected, and hence

---

[8]These set-up costs would consist primarily of the cost of acquiring athletic talent.

those arguments claiming incompatibility between athletic and economic competition are seen to be based upon an implicit acceptance of the existing monopoly structure.

In the absence of a more precise formulation of the model underlying the above argument, and without the specification of an explicit social welfare function, it is difficult to make rigorous statements concerning the welfare and efficiency aspects of this equilibrium. However, certain characteristics of the final equilibrium do lend themselves to normative interpretation.

Most arguments concerning public policy toward professional team sports implicitly assume that competitive equality among the teams in a league is desirable not only from the standpoint of the league's overall profitability, but also from the standpoint of the consumers of the product. Such an assumption seems appropriate if uncertainty of outcome increases the utility derived from viewing professional sports events. Also, there are by definition more potential winners in a close pennant race and, as implied by our empirical demand results, fan enjoyment appears to be increased through association with a potentially winning team. We will therefore accept the premise that equality of competition and close pennant races are desirable in a welfare sense.

As we have demonstrated above, the close pennant race is quite analogous to a public good. It is not likely to be regularly produced within the existing institutional framework of professional sports, a framework in which the distribution of athletic talent is determined by the decentralized decisions of independent profit maximizers operating in mutually exclusive monopoly markets of significantly varying strength. This conclusion holds with or without the existing set of restrictions on the mobility of athletic talent. On the other hand, when territorial rights are discarded and relatively free entry allowed, the market differences which are ultimately responsible for systematic inequality of athletic competition are themselves eliminated. Thus, on the criterion of equalizing playing strengths, it appears that a fully economically competitive organization of professional team sports would be superior to the present structure, as well as to a structure in which only the monopsony elements are eliminated.

Though it is not our purpose to develop all of the efficiency implications of the economically competitive equilibrium in professional sports, some remarks on this subject are warranted. The fully competitive model with unrestricted entry is clearly analogous to the Chamberlinian large group model with free entry. In each case products are differentiated and entry proceeds until pure profit opportunities are exhausted. As is well known, Chamberlin ([1956], pp. 104ff.) characterizes the equilibrium in such a market as one of "excess capacity" wherein prices exceed marginal production costs, and average costs are not at a minumum. More recently, Demsetz [1964] and Bishop [1967] have argued that the excess capacity theorem of Chamberlin is an oversimplification, and that, where product differentiation is possible, efficiency criteria should be based upon a broader interpretation of both demand and cost relationships. According to Demsetz ([1964], p. 639), "the proper measures for welfare economics are those that include differentiation costs and those that reflect the prices that buyers are willing to pay for differentiated products." On this basis, he concludes that minimization of the relevant average cost functions is possible in zero-profit equilibrium.

The analysis which we will employ in our discussion of competitive efficiency is similar to that of Demsetz, but differs in its conception of the relevant cost functions. It was initially developed by Professor James N. Rosse of Stanford University. He refers to this as the Transportation Cost–Imperfectly Competitive (TCIC) Model, in which the firm, in order to extend its market, must absorb the resulting increase in transportation costs. As Rosse points out, the model is considerably more general than the name implies, since transportation costs may be viewed as an analogue of general demand-increasing costs such as those incurred in advertising and product quality variation. The differences between this and the Demsetz approach will be pointed out as we proceed.

Let us rewrite the club's demand relation with price as the dependent variable. Thus we have

$$p = p(q,x), \tag{6-1}$$

where q is the number of seats sold and x is an index of the team's quality, and where $(\partial p/\partial q)<0$ and $(\partial p/\partial x)>0$. We assume also that the club's total costs, given by

$$c = c(q,x), \tag{6-2}$$

are increasing in both q and x.

The club will then be at maximum profit equilibrium when the following set of first order conditions are satisfied:

$$p + (\partial p/\partial q)q = \partial c/\partial q$$

$$(\partial p/\partial x)q = \partial c/\partial x. \tag{6-3}$$

These conditions may be interpreted as follows: For a given level of team quality, the marginal revenue from serving an additional consumer must be equal to the marginal cost of doing so; and for a given attendance level, the marginal revenue resulting from increased quality must equal the marginal cost of quality. These conditions may be solved for the optimal values of q and x, say (q^*,x^*), and thus, from (6-1), for p^*.

For a given price, let us define the *incremental cost* of serving an additional customer as the total derivative of the cost function with respect to q, namely

$$IC = (\partial c/\partial q) + (\partial c/\partial x)(dx/dq). \qquad (6\text{-}4)$$

Note that this is more than the simple notion of marginal cost, in that it explicitly includes the quality costs which must be undertaken if an additional consumer is to be served.[9] The term (dx/dq), the marginal rate of substitution between quality and attendance for a given price, may be obtained by equating to zero the total derivative of the demand equation. Thus

$$dx/dq = -\frac{\partial p/\partial q}{\partial p/\partial x}. \qquad (6\text{-}5)$$

If now the first order conditions (6-3) are solved for the ratio on the right side of (6-5) and the result substituted into the expression for incremental cost, we obtain the following:

$$IC = (\partial c/\partial q) + (\partial c/\partial x)\frac{p - \partial c/\partial q}{\partial c/\partial x} = p. \qquad (6\text{-}6)$$

Thus, when the club is maximizing profits, the price it charges for seats must be equal to the incremental cost of supplying those seats to additional consumers.

This model can be extended to a consideration of the excess capacity problem. In his approach, Chamberlin considered only average production costs, which are generated by varying q while holding x constant at x^*. His conclusion is that such an average cost figure will not be at a minimum in zero profit equilibrium. As we indicated above, Demsetz [1964] has shown that such a simplified concept of average cost is misleading, since a given point on the Chamberlinian average cost curve has relevance only for the assumed level of x. He suggests that for any output, total unit costs can be ascertained only by a simultaneous solution for the optimal p and x corresponding to that output. Demsetz argues that the average cost curve so generated may indeed have a minimum in zero profit equilibrium, though this is not necessarily the case, and he therefore rejects the excess capacity theorem as stated by Chamberlin.

Our approach is slightly different, and our conclusion stronger, than that of Demsetz. Suppose price is fixed at p^* and an average cost curve is generated as follows: As q is varied, x is chosen so that the corresponding level of q can be sold. It can easily be shown that the marginal curve associated with this type of

---

[9] This more general notion of marginal cost is also implicitly used by Noll and Okner [1971], p. 47. They in fact calculate its value for professional basketball to be approximately $2.50.

average cost is in fact the incremental cost as defined above in (6-6).[10] It then follows directly that in zero profit equilibrium, that is when $p = IC = AC$, the average cost curve described above must be at a minimum.

The situation is shown graphically in Figure 6-1. $AC(x^*)$ is the average cost

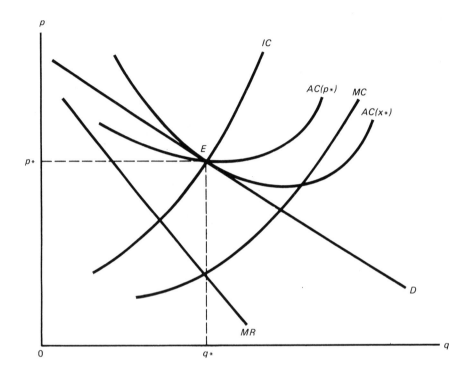

Figure 6-1.

---

[10]This can be shown in the following manner. Suppose $AC(= c/q)$ is generated by varying q and x simultaneously, while holding p fixed. Then, disregarding second order conditions, this AC is at a minimum (dAC/dq) = 0, or when

$$(dc/dq)\cdot q - c = 0$$

Since (dc/dq) = ($\partial c/\partial q$) + ($\partial c/\partial x$)$\cdot$(dx/dq) = IC, the condition above reduces to $IC = AC$.

curve employed by Chamberlin and is obtained by varying q while x is held constant at x^*. This curve is irrelevant for efficiency judgments, since values of q other than q^* cannot be sold unless either p or x is varied. $AC(p^*)$ is our average cost curve as defined above.

The firm is clearly in equilibrium at point E. Alterations in the quantity sold as a result of a price change produce simultaneous movements along $AC(x^*)$ and D, the demand curve. Such movements in either direction result in losses. Similarly, attempts to change q by changing x result in movements along $AC(p^*)$ and line Ep^*, and here also, losses are the result.

We conclude, therefore, that in the general model in which demand-increasing-costs exist, a model of which the professional sports industry is a special case, the excess capacity theorem is not warranted. In particular, when entry has driven pure profit to zero, the marginal consumer is paying the incremental cost of attracting him to a game, and the unit costs of providing the product at that price are at a minimum.

The effect of economic competition in both input and output markets on the salaries of professional athletes cannot be predicted a priori, since there could theoretically be forces operating both to increase and to decrease athletes' wages from their present levels. It is clear that if competitive bidding is introduced into the market for playing talent, while at the same time monopoly elements are retained in output markets, players' net wages will rise. The athlete's salary will bid up to equality with his marginal revenue product, while at the same time the burden of investment in the development of athletic skills will be shifted from the club to the player or to a third party, such as intercollegiate athletic programs.[11] The difference between the player's net wage (equal to marginal revenue product minus his share of investment in skill development) and his reservation price is economic rent, which now accrues to the player rather than to the club. For any given level of skill, the necessary investment will be less, and thus the rent larger, the greater the player's natural endowment of athletic talent.

Clearly, all players benefit from the introduction of competitive markets for their skills. However, once such competition is established, they also benefit from the existence of monopoly markets for outputs, since a portion of the resulting monopoly rents is captured by the players.[12] The athlete's marginal revenue product is greater if the club which employs him operates as a monopoly seller than if it faces competition in its output market, for in the latter case marginal revenue product would be calculated based upon a lower output price than under conditions of monopolized sale of output.

---

[11] The intercollegiate athletic system already provides this investment, to a large extent, in professional football and basketball. Baseball and hockey, which have much stricter reserve systems, rely primarily on investment in farm systems and minor league clubs for training players.

[12] This point is also made by Noll and Okner [1971], p. 49.

The total effect of economic competition in both input and output markets on the salaries of professional athletes is therefore theoretically unpredictable, depending upon such factors as the supply of athletic talent and the demand for professional sports entertainment. The more elastic the supply of playing skills and the less elastic the demand for output, the more likely are wages to fall, and conversely. Casual observation suggests that the supply elasticity may be larger than ordinarily anticipated, especially with respect to football and basketball talent. Though the true stars may be in short supply, there appears to be a surplus of average players developed annually by intercollegiate athletic programs. The fact that many athletes obtained in the player draft are relegated to "taxi" squads or released outright, only to eventually succeed with other clubs, seems to indicate that standards for judging athletic talent are quite uncertain and possibly even arbitrary, and that many more qualified players than are actually employed by professional clubs are developed in the colleges. Other than the historical accident of operating under much stricter reserve rules, there is no reason why baseball and hockey have not tapped this source of supply to the same extent as have football and basketball. Presumably they would if the reserve system were abolished.

At any rate, given these conflicting forces, the net effect on player salaries is ultimately an empirical question.

The Effects of Relaxing Some Assumptions

Thus far in our analysis of market results under full competitive conditions we have proceeded on the basis of some simplifying, and, in a few cases, perhaps unrealistic assumptions. We now examine the consequences of relaxing some of these assumptions.

First, we have implicitly ignored the fact that one of the basic production inputs, the team, is an indivisible entity defined by the conventions of the particular sport. With each club constrained to play all of its games in a single market area this "either-or" nature of the product may preclude long run equalization of market strengths. If, for example, supply and demand elasticities determine that the minimum market population consistent with normal returns is one million, those markets with 1.5 million population will be served in equilibrium by only a single club whose optimal quality is greater than those of clubs locating in markets whose population is an integer multiple of one million. The larger this minimum profitable market size, the greater the possibility of significant differences in market strength in final equilibrium.[13]

There is, however, no logical necessity for each club to play all of its home games in a single metropolitan area. If the club can divide its "home" schedule among a number of different local markets, the problem of team indivisibility

[13] See Table 2-1 in Chapter 2.

will be effectively eliminated. Markets whose size or strength is not an integer multiple of the economically viable minimum will be served by one or more clubs playing fractional parts of their total schedule. Such a practice has, in fact, been undertaken by many members of the relatively new American Basketball Association. Faced with the apparent dilemma of having either to compete with the NBA clubs in the major population areas, or being relegated to the remaining smaller markets, many ABA franchises have become statewide or regional in their scheduling, playing parts of their schedule in each of a number of smaller population centers in their region.

Another problem with which we have not dealt, and which might theoretically preclude the stability of the competitive equilibrium described above, is the possibility of profit functions that are nonconcave over a significant range of variations in team quality. More specifically, if the marginal net returns from the employment of athletic talent are not decreasing for each club when the industry is in equilibrium, then that equilibrium will not be stable. A necessary condition for this type of instability is that either the marginal revenue product of athletic talent is increasing or the marginal cost of athletic talent is decreasing; a sufficient condition is that both of these simultaneously hold.

Whether either or both of these conditions are met is ultimately an empirical question, but there seems to be no a priori reason to expect that the marginal revenue product of athletic talent is increasing. On the other hand, given the existing system of explicit rewards for winning, along with a plausible assumption about the formation of expectations on the part of professional athletes, there may be factors exerting a downward pressure on the cost of acquiring additional athletic talent as the quality of the team increases. If for example, victory this year by the Dodgers produces expectations among players that such is likely to be the case again next year (whether or not these expectations are valid *ex ante*), and if there are rewards to victorious players either in the form of direct playoff money or indirect benefits, then the Dodgers will find that their cost of attracting additional units of athletic talent will fall. More talent will be purchased, the club is more likely to win again, and the expectations are essentially likely to be self-fulfilling and self-reinforcing. The process will continue only until either marginal costs begin to rise or marginal revenue product falls more sharply than marginal cost; but our conclusion must be, that if such pecuniary scale economies exist, the equality of athletic competition may not be a characteristic of stable league equilibrium.

One possible solution to this problem, that of eliminating or lowering direct rewards to winning players, carries with it a dilemma: The integrity of athletic competition, and thus the primary attraction of sport, is insured when players are clearly and explicitly motivated to win by direct and visible economic incentives. The interest of the fan is directly related to the stakes of the game, and if these stakes are diminished the sport loses part of its appeal. This is perhaps why professional sports leagues, otherwise reluctant to provide any information concerning the financial aspects of their operations, take great pains to publicize the winning and losing shares for athletes involved in playoff championships.

Therefore, a more equal sharing of playoff revenues among winners and losers, even though it would reduce the likelihood of instability, may not be feasible as an overall solution to the problem, and an alternate approach may be required. One possibility is to make player expectations regarding future team performance less elastic with respect to past performance.

In any case, it is clear that some collective action on the part of league members may be necessary if this problem is to be internalized. We may not be able to rely solely on decentralization and competitive pressures to insure an equilibrium characterized by relative equality of athletic strengths.[14]

If the problems discussed in the immediately preceding sections do not in fact arise, or if they can be easily resolved, then the competitive solution discussed above provides an economically efficient recommendation for public policy toward professional sports. However, it is important that we recognize, that the economic competition of which we are speaking must still take place within a set of unique institutional constraints necessitated by the peculiarities of the industry's production process. In a sense, what we have done is to minimize, not render null, that set of constraints.

The complex nature of the production process requires the cooperation of otherwise independent economic entities: Unrestricted economic competition, or that bounded only by the traditional legal and economic constraints of strictly decentralized laissez-faire organization are probably not sufficient, in the case of professional team sports, to make the provision of this service economically efficient or even feasible. In particular, certain areas must remain the subject of collective (league) resolution if production is to be efficient. Note that they all derive directly from the fact that all aspects of the product must be jointly produced by two or more clubs, and do not constitute what we would consider collusion in the usual sense.[15]

Due to certain interdependencies in the production process it is probably neither feasible nor desirable to allow completely free, frictionless entry by new clubs. Rather, certain of the peculiar interdependencies in a professional sports league would require some collective control over entry.

First, and most obviously, it must be the league's function to standardize the product through the adoption of a uniform set of definitions, playing rules, and

---

[14]Whether or not the conditions exist which might lead to these theoretical problems is of course an empirical question. A priori, however, we feel that the necessary conditions (namely, marginal costs declining at a faster rate than marginal revenues) are not likely to be encountered in practice.

[15]An analogy might be drawn here to the automobile industry. Joint agreement by all auto makers on a standard bumper height would reduce driving costs and would hardly be considered collusive, but rather an efficient solution to an externality problem.

so forth. Presumably, therefore, one requirement for entry must be the acceptance of these rules by the potential entrant.

Secondly, because the quality of a new league member affects demand conditions for all of the existing clubs, it appears desirable for the league to define and enforce minimum acceptable quality criteria. Due to the joint nature of the production process, there might otherwise be some incentive for the formation and entry of very poor quality teams.

As an extreme example, it is probably true that a sandlot baseball team could earn enough revenue to cover its costs if it scheduled a game against the New York Yankees in Yankee stadium. It is obvious that if such a practice became widespread, the legitimacy of athletic competition and thus the very existence of the professional sport would be threatened. The primary economic appeal of major league professional sports is vested in the superiority of the product they supply, and this aspect of the product may require protection by the league.

Scheduling is also an area in which collective action is essential, and which might conceivably serve as a minor barrier to perfectly free entry. The potential entrant must be worked into the time-travel schedules of already existing league members, and the transaction costs involved in reaching some new accord might be covered by an entry fee.

Entry by a new club might also be contingent upon a prior announcement of its intentions, in order to give the league an opportunity to revise any existing schedule. This of course presumes that the potential entrant has already demonstrated its ability to meet the other entry criteria outlined above, thus justifying the costs of schedule revision.

Other considerations arise with respect to the mobility of athletic talent. Unrestricted movement of players among teams is probably not feasible from a practical standpoint, since it could conceivably generate substantial adverse effects. Club owners have always argued, for example, that two such effects are (1) the potential destruction of team continuity from season to season, and (2) the threat to the integrity of the athletic competition on which the sport's economic appeal is ultimately based.

Fears regarding the effects on continuity, which is presumably a requirement for fan identification with the team, seem to be unfounded. The extent to which continuity of team personnel exists is certainly subject to the internal decision process of the club, and as such may be purchased much as any other productive input. Specifically the club could provide wage incentives to veteran players. Any discontinuities resulting from a large-scale shift of players among clubs are likely to be a short-term phenomenon, associated with adjustment to equilibrium, rather than a normal state of affairs.

The potential effects of absolutely free mobility on player incentives, and the implication of these effects for the integrity of athletic competition cannot be so lightly dismissed. As an illustration of the difficulties which might arise, consider the following: A player, still nominally employed by the Dodgers, is simultaneously negotiating with the Giants. If the two teams are to meet in an important game, the player's "loyalties" must be divided. In particular, although he is nominally playing for the Dodgers, it is clearly in his economic interest that the Giants win, if there is a good chance that he may soon be playing for them.

This situation, and others similar to it, necessitate at least some minimal restrictions on the mobility of playing talent among members of the league. First, the contract between the club and the player must be binding over at least the course of the playing season. Secondly, bargaining between players and clubs should be prohibited during the playing season. It must be left to the league to enforce these and any other justifiable restrictions on player mobility.

Our general conclusion is that, within an appropriate set of collectively enforced institutional constraints necessitated by the unique joint nature of the production process, the existence of economically competitive input and output markets could constitute a viable and efficient market structure for professional team sports. Both the allocative inefficiency and distributional inequity which characterize the present monopoly-monopsony structure would be largely eliminated and the "quality" of the product improved through greater long run equalization of playing strengths among clubs.

Some Recommendations for a "Second Best" Policy

Unfortunately, given the present political environment, neither the elimination of the league's monopoly control over entry, and thus over total supply, nor the abolition of territorial rights seems to be a realistically attainable goal for public policy. League cartels are strongly entrenched in all sports but basketball and hockey, and in the case of basketball, Congressional approval of the proposed merger of the two competing leagues seems imminent.

Pragmatism therefore requires that we address ourselves to the problem of policy formulation when the existence of monopoly restrictions on the output side of the market are accepted as inevitable. Our previous analysis suggests the following recommendations.[16]

First, with regard to markets for athletic talent, the reserve clause as a perpetual option on a player's services should be eliminated. It should be replaced with, at most, a modified reserve system whereby a player is bound by a contract of perhaps a year or longer. Though this latter system nominally exists at present in both professional football and basketball, its substantive effects are minimized by an "indemnity" arrangement requiring that the club losing the services of a player who has "played out his option" be compensated by the club which acquires his services.[17] This indemnity system should be

---

[16]Some of these recommendations have been made by other writers. See for example Rottenberg [1956], and Noll and Okner [1971].

[17]See Chapter 2.

abolished on the grounds that it effectively eliminates a player's bargaining position by reducing his alternate marginal productivity, and as such its effects are nearly the same as those of the perpetual reservation system.

We propose that, once a player has fulfilled all of the obligations of his contract, he become a "free agent" in the true sense, unconstrained by any monopsony restrictions on his mobility. The player draft system should also be either eliminated or modified to allow for competitive bidding by the clubs for the services of new athletes.

As our model has shown, implementation of these recommendations alone will not eliminate the tendency toward long run inequality of team playing strengths which results in the existence of unprofitable franchises. Therefore, to insure the viability of the league once restrictions on player mobility have been eliminated, it is necessary that policies be adopted which will tend to equalize the revenue potential of all clubs in a league. This might be accomplished by league action to relocate franchises in a way that more accurately reflects market population. For example, New York might have four clubs, Chicago and Los Angeles two clubs each, Cincinnati one club, and so on.

Other approaches might include a more equal division of gate shares between the home club and the visiting club, or the mutual pooling of broadcast revenues. As we have shown,[18] a more equal division of live gate revenues tends to smooth out differences in market strength, and in so doing encourages greater equality in the distribution of athletic talent. The club's effective market becomes a weighted average of its own market and those of the other clubs in the league. Up to a point, increasing the visitor's share of the gate tends to reduce the effect of intermarket differences on revenue potential, by diminishing the weight the club places on its own market. In fact, where the schedule is symmetric, in the sense that each club plays the same number of home and away games and the same number of games against each of the other league members, the value of the visitor's gate share which completely equalizes effective market strengths is independent of these strengths and equal to $(n - 1)/n$, where n is the number of teams in the league.[19] Note, however, that the visitor's share would be larger than that of the home team, and collective agreement on such a scheme would probably be unlikely.

A similar argument applies to the sharing of broadcast revenues, especially those derived from the televising of games, since market strength differentials are also reflected in variations in revenue potential from this source.

Casual empiricism suggests the potential effectiveness of these measures.

---

[18] See Chapter 4.

[19] To show this, let v be the visitor's share of the gate and let m be the number of home (and road) games played by any club against each of the other clubs in the league. Then if s_i is an index of the strength of the i-th club's home market, its "effective" market strength, S_i, will be a weighted average of all markets, namely, $S_i = (1 - v)(n - 1)ms_i + vm\left(\sum_{j \neq i} s_j\right)$. It can then be shown that the solution, for v, of $S_i = S_k$ is independent of both s_i and s_j and is given by $v = (n - 1)/n$.

Among the four professional team sports, the National Football League has engaged in revenue sharing to a much greater extent than baseball, basketball, or hockey. In the NFL, live gate shares are divided on a 60-40 basis and all television revenues are pooled and shared equally by all league members. Contrast this with professional baseball where the visitor's share of the gate is 20 percent, and with professional basketball and hockey where the visitor's share is virtually zero. Also in baseball, though the proceeds of the national television rights are pooled, each club retains the revenues from its local television contracts. In 1973 for example, this resulted in over $2.5 million for the Los Angeles Dodgers, compared with less than $1.4 million for the Milwaukee Brewers.[20]

Possibly as a result of this revenue sharing, competitive equality seems to be much more of a reality in professional football than in the other professional sports. This in turn is reflected in the rapid increase in the value of NFL franchises relative to the value of franchises in other sports.[21]

It might also be desirable, from a "second best" point of view, to encourage the development of strong players' associations. The argument in favor of this is based primarily on distributional or equity considerations, in that, given the monopoly position of the clubs, the establishment of "countervailing power" in their labor markets would redistribute some of the monopoly profits to the professional athletes.[22] However, where units of labor are highly differentiated, as in professional sports, collective bargaining will be much more difficult than where labor is relatively homogeneous. Since skills and hence productivity levels differ significantly among professional athletes, collective wage settlements are almost certainly precluded. For this reason, players' associations, where they exist, usually focus their economic power on such matters as pension plans and playing conditions, and leave direct salary negotiation to the individual player. It is in this "fringe benefit" area, therefore, that the distributional effects of players' unions will be primarily felt.

The clubs of course can be predicted to vigorously oppose collectivization by the players, but as the recent strike by major league baseball players has demonstrated, a trend toward unionization among professional athletes may be gathering momentum.

Some Observations on Joint Profit Maximization

Collective agreement among league members is clearly required to determine and to enforce any revenue sharing arrangement. If, as our analysis seems to imply,

---

[20]See Chapter 2.

[21]See Table 2-2.

[22]See Galbraith [1952], especially Chapter 9. On a much more theoretical level, there may also be an argument for this on allocational grounds. As Lipsey and Lancaster [1956] and others have recognized, when certain elements of an economic system are monopolized, then it is not necessarily optimal in an efficiency sense to have the remainder of the system or any of its particular sectors organized competitively.

this might lead to an increase in total league profits, the question must be asked as to why such agreements do not exist on a greater scale in professional team sports, especially baseball. Here, it would seem, is an industry whose privileged status under the antitrust statutes endows it with a unique opportunity to pursue maximum joint profits, but where available evidence suggests that at least some of these opportunities have been neglected.

As we have repeatedly emphasized, attempts to promote competitive equality, either through equalization of effective market strengths or by direct reallocation of athletic talent, are by themselves not likely to be met with unanimous acceptance by league members. In particular, the clubs located in the stronger markets would oppose these schemes, which would result in lower profits for them and thus a fall in the capitalized value of their franchises. If it is true, therefore, that total league profits would increase, the question then reduces to the ability of the league to institute a comprehensive and enforceable system of side payments in order to compensate the clubs in the strong markets. Although it is not our intention to analyze this side payment problem in great depth, some suggestions are warranted concerning the possible difficulties that attempts to establish such a system might encounter.

The first difficulty arises from the nature of the product itself. It is possible that the clubs feel that visible and explicit economic cooperation among league members might compromise the facade of competition from which sport derives its ultimate appeal. If this competitive posture is to be maintained, it may necessitate at least nominal economic independence among the members of the league. Such an argument, however, overlooks the possibility of more covert methods of profit sharing, and in itself certainly does not provide a complete explanation of the apparent lack of perfect collusion with the league.

Perhaps more important is the uncertainty with which the clubs may regard the effects of policies designed to increase competitive equality. Our model suggests the rational course of action only on the assumption of complete information regarding the possible outcomes of various strategies, and the absence of such information may preclude the league's ability to pursue jointly optimal behavior.[23] Specifically, if the rich market clubs are risk averse, they may reject an uncertain future payoff in favor of their present profit situation, unless the expected value of future net gains is relatively large. Similarly, the poor market clubs will not support a system of side payments in which they must assume an uncertain burden, and the possibility of net loss. In such a case the two sides may reach an impasse.

Conclusion

In conclusion, let us summarize the major findings of this analysis and review their implications for an enlightened policy toward the professional team sports industry.

[23]These effects of the lack of information on the possibilities for collusive activity are widely recognized. See, for example, Fellner [1949], Chapter 3, and Shubik [1959], Chapter 8.

First, we have noted a strong positive correlation between economic performance and athletic performance: Potentially winning teams, teams which are in
pennant contention, are generally more profitable than losing teams. The actual
distribution of relative athletic strength, and thus of profits, is in turn the
outcome of the set of simultaneous input decisions of the independent
profit-maximizing clubs. We have shown that such a distribution will not
generally be one of long run sporting equality among clubs, but rather will be
influenced by variations in the strength of the respective markets in which the
clubs are located. There will be a long run tendency for clubs located in the
strong markets to be both economically and sportingly superior to those clubs
located in weak markets.

We have shown also that the present institutional restrictions on the
economic mobility of professional athletes, as embodied in the various forms of
the reserve systems, are neither necessary nor sufficient conditions for eliminating the tendency to long run competitive inequality within a league. Rather
these institutions serve as a rent transfer mechanism, assuring the economic
viability of the league at the expense of the players.

We have therefore concluded that the reserve system is an inequitable
institution, which is furthermore incapable óf accomplishing its ostensible
purpose of equalizing athletic strength. We contend that it should be abolished
and replaced by an attempt to eliminate, or at least mitigate, the basic market
differentials which are ultimately responsible for the tendency toward inequality
in sporting competition.

An ideal solution appears to be the elimination of barriers to economic
competition on the output side of the market as well as on the input side,
though certain types of collective activity would still be required of the league.
In general, those exogenous intermarket differences which prevent the equalization of playing strengths would tend to be eroded by natural market forces,
while at the same time the allocative inefficiencies and distributive inequities
associated with the exercise of market power would be reduced or eliminated.
Though the validity of this contention rests upon certain assumptions about the
behavioral and technological relations with which the industry is confronted, it
is a priori a straightforward solution to the policy problem.

Unfortunately, such a proposal is not likely to win acceptance by either
owners or players, and thus we have suggested some more pragmatic proposals
for mitigating the effects of intermarket differences. These include a more equal
division of ticket revenues, more equal sharing of broadcast revenues, the
distribution of franchises according to market population, and the development
of stronger players' associations. The adoption of any or all of these proposals
should be accompanied by either the complete abrogation or substantial
alteration of the present reserve and draft systems.

The analysis developed and applied in this book has by no means exhausted
the potential contributions of economic analysis as applied to the professional

team sports industry. Rather, we have focused on a particular set of institutions which are unique to this industry, and at the same time are a subject of current legal and economic controversy. It is our hope that the result is a clearer understanding of the economic forces involved, and a basis for the resolution of these controversies in an enlightened and rational manner.

Bibliography

Bibliography

Alchian, Armen A. (1950). "Uncertainty, Evolution and Economic Theory." JOURNAL OF POLITICAL ECONOMY. (June: pp. 211-21).

Allen, Lee. (1961). THE NATIONAL LEAGUE STORY. (New York: Hill and Wang).

Andreano, Ralph. (1965). NO JOY IN MUDVILLE—THE DILEMMA OF MAJOR LEAGUE BASEBALL. (Cambridge: Schenkman Publishing Co.).

Archibald, G.C. (1964). "Profit Maximizing and Non-Price Competition." ECONOMICA. (February: pp. 13-22).

Baumol, William J., and Bowen, William G. (1966). THE PERFORMING ARTS—AN ECONOMIC DILEMMA. (New York: The Twentieth Century Fund).

Becker, Gary S. (1964). HUMAN CAPITAL. (New York: Columbia University Press for National Bureau of Economic Research).

Bishop, Robert L. (1960). "Duopoly: Collusion or Warfare?" AMERICAN ECONOMIC REVIEW. (December: pp. 933-61).

Bishop, Robert L. (1967). "Monopolistic Competition and Welfare Economics." Chapter 11 in Kuenne (ed.), MONOPOLISTIC COMPETITION THEORY. (New York: Wiley).

Buchanan, James M., and Tullock, Gordon. (1965). THE CALCULUS OF CONSENT. Ann Arbor Paperbacks. (Ann Arbor: The University of Michigan Press).

Chamberlin, Edward H. (1953). "The Product as an Economic Variable." QUARTERLY JOURNAL OF ECONOMICS. (February: pp. 1-29).

Chamberlin, Edward H. (1956). THE THEORY OF MONOPOLISTIC COMPE-TITION. Seventh ed. (Cambridge: Harvard University Press).

Christ, Carl F. (1966). ECONOMETRIC MODELS AND METHODS. (New York: Wiley).

Craig, Jack. (1971). "Cutback in Slow Motion Replays." THE SPORTING NEWS. (July 24: p. 13).

Davenport, David S. (1969). "Collusive Competition in Major League Baseball: Its Theory and Institutional Development." AMERICAN ECONOMIST. (Fall: pp. 6-30).

Demsetz, Harold. (1959). "The Nature of Equilibrium in Monopolistic Compe-tition." JOURNAL OF POLITICAL ECONOMY. (February: pp. 21-30).

Demsetz, Harold. (1964). "The Welfare and Empirical Implications of Monopo-listic Competition." THE ECONOMIC JOURNAL. (September: pp. 623-41).

Dorfman, Robert, and Steiner, Peter O. (1954). "Optimal Advertising and Optimal Quality." AMERICAN ECONOMIC REVIEW. (December: pp. 827-36).

Durso, Joseph. (1971). THE ALL AMERICAN DOLLAR—THE BIG BUSINESS OF SPORTS. (Boston: Houghton-Mifflin).

El-Hodiri, Mohamed, and Quirk, James. (1971). "An Economic Model of a Professional Sports League." JOURNAL OF POLITICAL ECONOMY. (November/December: pp. 1302-19).

Fellner, William J. (1949). COMPETITION AMONG THE FEW. Reprinted. (New York: Augustus M. Kelley, 1960).

Ferguson, C.E. (1972). MICROECONOMIC THEORY. Third ed. (Homewood, Illinois: Irwin).

Fisher, Franklin M. (1962). A PRIORI INFORMATION AND TIME SERIES ANALYSIS. Contributions to Economic Analysis, Vol. XXVI. (Amsterdam: North-Holland).

Flood, Curt. (1971). THE WAY IT IS. (New York: Trident Press).

FORBES. (1971). "Who Says Baseball is Like Ballet?" (April 1: pp. 24-31).

Friedman, J.W. (1968). "Reaction Functions and the Theory of Duopoly." REVIEW OF ECONOMIC STUDIES. (July: pp. 201-208).

Friedman, Milton. (1953). "The Methodology of Positive Economics." Chapter 1 in ESSAYS IN POSITIVE ECONOMICS. (Chicago: University of Chicago Press).

Galbraith, John Kenneth. (1952). AMERICAN CAPITALISM. (Boston: Houghton-Mifflin).

Gorman, W.M. (1964). "More Scope for Qualitative Economics." REVIEW OF ECONOMIC STUDIES. (January: pp. 65-68).

Gregory, Paul. (1956). THE BASEBALL PLAYER: AN ECONOMIC STUDY. (Washington, D.C.: Public Affairs Press).

Henderson, James M., and Quandt, Richard E. (1971). MICROECONOMIC THEORY—A MATHEMATICAL APPROACH. Second ed. (New York: McGraw-Hill).

Hicks, J.R. (1946). VALUE AND CAPITAL. Second ed. (London: The Clarendon Press).

Horowitz, Ira. (1970). "Nondogmatic Conjectures in a Cournot Market." WESTERN ECONOMIC JOURNAL. (March: pp. 73-85).

Johnston, J. (1960). ECONOMETRIC METHODS. (New York: McGraw-Hill).

Jones, J.C.H. (1969). "The Economics of the National Hockey League." CANADIAN JOURNAL OF ECONOMICS. (February: pp. 1-20).

Koch, James V. (1971). "The Economics of 'Big Time' Intercollegiate Athletics." SOCIAL SCIENCES QUARTERLY. (September: pp. 248-60).

Koppet, Leonard. (1967). A THINKING MAN'S GUIDE TO BASEBALL. (New York: E.P. Dutton).

Koppet, Leonard. (1972). "Draft is Vital . . . In Holding Down Salaries." THE SPORTING NEWS. (March 25: p. 4).

Lancaster, Kelvin. (1962). "The Scope of Qualitative Economics." REVIEW OF ECONOMIC STUDIES. (January: pp. 99-123).

Lancaster, Kelvin. (1966). "The Solution of Qualitative Comparative Static Systems." QUARTERLY JOURNAL OF ECONOMICS. (May: pp. 278-95).

Lieb, Frederick G. (1944a). CONNIE MACK. (New York: G.P. Putnam).

Lieb, Frederick G. (1944b). THE ST. LOUIS CARDINALS. (New York: G.P. Putnam).

Lipsey, R.G., and Lancaster, Kelvin. (1956). "The General Theory of Second Best." REVIEW OF ECONOMIC STUDIES. (December: pp. 11-32).

Mann, Arthur. (1957). BRANCH RICKEY: AMERICAN IN ACTION. (Boston: Houghton-Mifflin).

Meany, Tom. (1953). THE ARTFUL DODGERS. (New York: A.S. Barnes).

Monahan, Leo. (1971). "The Rich Get Richer." THE SPORTING NEWS. (June 19: p. 53).

Neale, Walter C. (1964). "The Peculiar Economics of Professional Sports." QUARTERLY JOURNAL OF ECONOMICS. (February: pp. 1-14).

Noll, Roger G., and Okner, Benjamin A. (1971). Statement Before the Subcommittee on Antitrust and Monopoly Legislation of the Senate Judiciary Committee on S.2373, The Basketball Merger Bill. (September 23).

Ogle, Jim. (1971). "Gibb's Case Pinpoints Yankee Failure to Rebuild." THE SPORTING NEWS. (July 10: p. 3).

Pascal, Anthony H., and Rapping, Leonard A. (1970). RACIAL DISCRIMINATION IN ORGANIZED BASEBALL. (RM-6227-RC). The Rand Corporation.

Robinson, Joan. (1933). THE ECONOMICS OF IMPERFECT COMPETITION. Reprinted. (London: Macmillan, 1959).

Rottenberg, Simon. (1956). "The Baseball Players' Labor Market." JOURNAL OF POLITICAL ECONOMY. (June: pp. 242-58).

Samuelson, Paul A. (1947). FOUNDATIONS OF ECONOMIC ANALYSIS. Reprinted. (New York: Atheneum, 1965).

Shubik, Martin. (1959). STRATEGY AND MARKET STRUCTURE. (New York: Wiley).

Smith, Lester. (1972). "Playoff, Series Revenues Put O's in Black in '71." THE SPORTING NEWS. (April 15: p. 9).

THE SPORTING NEWS. (1971). "A Blessing for the Rich." Editorial. (June 19: p. 15).

THE SPORTING NEWS. (1972). "Sports Payrolls Examined." (April 8: p. 46).

Stellini, Vito. (1971). "Sports Rank as High Risk Investment." THE SPORTING NEWS. (May 8: p. 42).

Stigler, G.J. (1966). THE THEORY OF PRICE. (New York: Macmillan).

Suits, Daniel B. (1957). "Use of Dummy Variables in Regression Equations." JOURNAL OF THE AMERICAN STATISTICAL ASSOCIATION. (December: pp. 548-51).

United States Congress. (1957). House. ORGANIZED PROFESSIONAL TEAM SPORTS. Hearings Before the Antitrust Subcommittee. Parts 1-3. 85th Congress. First session.

United States Congress. (1964). Senate. PROFESSIONAL SPORTS ANTITRUST BILL—1964. Hearings Before the Subcommittee on Antitrust and Monopoly. 88th Congress. Second session.

Veeck, Bill. (1967). THE HUSTLER'S HANDBOOK. (New York: G.P. Putnam).

Voigt, David Quentin. (1970). AMERICAN BASEBALL. Vol. 2. (Norman: University of Oklahoma Press).

Wonnacott, Ronald J., and Wonnacott, Thomas H. (1970). ECONOMETRICS. (New York: Wiley).

Data Sources:

The American League of Professional Baseball Clubs. AMERICAN LEAGUE REDBOOK. (1950-1970).

The National League of Professional Baseball Clubs. NATIONAL LEAGUE GREENBOOK. (1950-1970).

OFFICIAL BASEBALL GUIDE. (1950-1970). (St. Louis: THE SPORTING NEWS).

SALES MANAGEMENT. (1950-1970). "Annual Survey of Buying Power." (Second June Issue).

THE SPORTING NEWS. (1950-1970). (Various Issues).

United States Department of Commerce. Bureau of the Census. STATISTICAL ABSTRACT OF THE UNITED STATES: 1970. (91st ed.). (Washington, D.C.: U.S. Government Printing Office).

United States Deparmtent of Labor. Bureau of Labor Statistics. HANDBOOK OF LABOR STATISTICS: 1970. (Washington, D.C.: U.S. Government Printing Office).

Index

105

About the Author

Henry G. Demmert was born in 1943 in Los Angeles, California. He received the B.S. in 1965 from the University of Santa Clara, graduating with honors. He did his graduate work, as an NDEA Fellow, at Stanford University, earning the Ph.D. in economics in June 1972. Dr. Demmert has been an Assistant Professor of Economics at the University of Santa Clara since 1968.